"This book will refresh weary moms in their glorious task of raising their children to know and love Jesus. Motherhood draws on deep resources that must be refilled regularly. Deb Weakly and her Help Club for Moms team do just that—they pour into us so that we have something to pour out to our children. This resource is full of Scripture, prayers, personal stories, honest reflection, and practical encouragement. It not only brings strength and hope but also invites you into a community of mothers who care deeply about the things that matter most."

Dr. Michelle Anthony
executive pastor, Family Ministries, New Life Church, Colorado Springs

"I'm *so thankful* for the Help Club for Moms! This amazing community helps me through a new transition in life with two little ones. They say it takes a village to raise kids...I say it takes a Help Club!"

Rachael Bamfield
member of the Help Club for Moms at New Life Church, Colorado Springs

"*The Help Club for Moms* is a tangible expression of what can occur through vision, hard work, collaboration, and prayer. I have had the privilege of seeing this 'wise woman' approach in action. Every woman needs someone to understand what she's going through. Deb Weakly and her prayerful team not only understand but roll up their sleeves to come alongside you. This is your go-to resource for raising children!"

Yvette Maher
chief development officer, Dream Centers

"*The Help Club for Moms* is a timely book that speaks directly to the needs and desires of a woman's heart. Deb Weakly and her team embody the very word *passion* as they write out of a deep well that is both practical and profoundly wise. Readers will feel safe in being who they are while also embracing the wisdom found in these pages."

Stephanie Henderson
executive pastor, Women, Media, and Communications, New Life Church, Colorado Springs

D1498847

"Help Club for Moms is a precious ministry helping thousands of women live out their God-given vocation as mothers. I am so thankful for this new resource, which is sure to become your trusted companion as you walk faithfully with Jesus in taking care of the little ones He's entrusted to you."

Andrew Arndt
associate and teaching pastor, New Life Church, Colorado Springs

"Do you need some friends who understand your everyday challenges, celebrations, and conundrums? *The Help Club for Moms* contains a wealth of wisdom, distilled from women just like you who want to be the best moms they can be. Start from the beginning or jump right to what you care most about. This resource can change how you experience your days with your kids and those in your world. It is filled with heartfelt, practical, Spirit-led encouragement you can use. Come join the club!"

Dr. Cheryl L. Meredith
chief ideation officer, Navigators Workplace

"The Help Club for Moms is fabulous!"

David Eaton
president and cofounder, Axis Student Ministries

"The Help Club for Moms has a profound and powerful vision and is impacting lives on the other side of the world. Love Jesus Church in Capetown, South Africa, believes in the program and is grateful for the opportunity to participate. Through the Help Club for Moms, we believe families will be changed and churches will be strengthened in Cape Town."

Kacy Ladd
women's ministry director, Love Jesus Church, Cape Town, South Africa

"*The Help Club for Moms* is a cup of cold water in the marathon of motherhood. Moms sharing from their experiences, misfires, mishaps, and milestones spill forth on these pages. Their ideas and encouragement are relatable and personal. This book will help fuel your passion for Jesus through the work of the Holy Spirit in your parenting. May you feast on what this gifted group brings to the table!"

Blythe Daniel
author of *Mended: Restoring the Hearts of Mothers and Daughters*

THE
Help Club
FOR
Moms

Deb Weakly
and the Help Club for Moms Team

HARVEST HOUSE PUBLISHERS
EUGENE, OREGON

Scripture versions used are listed on page 218.

Cover design by Kara Klontz Design

Cover photo by Connie Gabbert

Interior design by Chad Dougherty

Interior image by Barbara A Lane from Pixabay

Author photos © Jacqueline Hall

The Help Club for Moms

Copyright © 2020 by The Help Club for Moms
Published by Harvest House Publishers
Eugene, Oregon 97408
www.harvesthousepublishers.com

ISBN 978-0-7369-7873-6 (pbk.)
ISBN 978-0-7369-7874-3 (eBook)

Library of Congress Cataloging-in-Publication Data is on file at the Library of Congress, Washington, DC.

Printed in the United States of America

20 21 22 23 24 25 26 27 28 / VP-CD / 10 9 8 7 6 5 4 3 2 1

This book is humbly dedicated to our precious

Lord and Savior, Jesus Christ.

We love You with our whole hearts
and are forever grateful for Your amazing love.
May You be glorified through every word,
and may Your kingdom grow with each heart You touch.

WE THANK GOD FOR...

Our husbands, who have supported us every step of the way: Randy Weakly, Kim Mast, Kassidy Carson, Bill Davis, Hugh Jones, Adam Porter, Brian Sanders, Todd Valdois, Luke Willis, and Larry Lain.

Daphne Close, Heather Doolittle, Leslie Leonard, and Tara Fox, your patience, wisdom, and loving labor helped form the foundations of the Help Club for Moms. God has used your faith to reach thousands of women around the world for the gospel of Jesus Christ. Amanda Hennessey, Ashley Hughes, Danielle Novotny, Elise Turner, Gabby Campbell, Jackie Hall, Janelle Folz, Karen Behnke, Karolyn Dicken, Kathryn Egly, Kristi Valentine, Linda Steppenbacker, Michelle Hammers, Rachel Kindervater, Rebecca Bornman, Rebekah Measmer, Stephanie Sandretto, and Tonya Baldessari, thank you for sharing your individual gifts with the Help Club for Moms. You help make our ministry so beautiful! Joan and Tom Weakly, thank you for your generous gifts, which helped us launch the ministry. And a special thank you to our family ministry pastor, Dr. Michelle Anthony. You have always believed in the mission of Help Club for Moms. We love you!

Bob and Emilie Barnes, thank you for sharing your love and timeless wisdom with the next generation of parents. We are a product of your ministry and your great love for Jesus Christ. We carry the baton to this next generation on your shoulders. We are so grateful for you!

To all our precious Help Club for Moms sisters, we thank God for you and are honored to know you, either in person or online or through our books. We count it a joy to walk this road of motherhood with you.

Contents

Part 4: The Wise Woman Creates a Home

Part 5: The Wise Woman Fosters Friendships

Part 6: HELPful Resources

Mama, Do You Need Help?

KRYSTLE PORTER

Hello, sweet friend, we are so glad you are here! Chances are you picked up this book and are looking for a little help. Maybe you are weary from one too many restless nights with your baby, tired over toddler tantrums, worn out from the hustle and bustle of an impossibly busy family schedule, or struggling through the teen years that leave you overwhelmed and looking for a break. Whatever season of mothering you are in, we want to begin by saying there *is* help for you. There is hope for all of us!

Though this book is filled to the brim with tried-and-true articles and resources for you to navigate motherhood a bit easier, our one and only help is found in the Holy Spirit—Jesus who lives inside of us. Before we can claim to ever be a help to you, we must begin our journey at the source of true help! Jesus is the source of our help, and He patiently waits for us, His precious believers, to call on Him. He wants us to allow the Holy Spirit into every crack and crevice of our hearts so we can hear directly from Him. He wants to shine a light into the dark, hidden spaces of our souls and refresh us with the hope and comfort we long for.

9

In motherhood, the day-in and day-out routines and chores can feel incredibly mundane. Many days can go by where we feel unnoticed and underappreciated. But there is good news: God sees us. He sees each and every tiny detail of our days. He knows the number of spills you have cleaned up and the number of diapers you have changed. He sees the tears you have cried (or held in) and cares deeply for each and every one. The job of raising children is not an easy task, but it is a holy calling. With God's help, we know that we can step outside of our human limitations and step into God's strength and joy as we approach each new day. He is able to renew us and energize us as no one else can.

We would never presume to know your family's unique puzzle; however, Jesus does. We urge you to never forget the powerful help you have access to each and every day through the Holy Spirit. Never underestimate the power that lives inside of you as a Christ-follower, and never forget that you can personally and intimately hear from Jesus on your family's behalf. Ask the Holy Spirit for help in your marriage, with your kids, and in any other area where you have a need. Allow yourself to be known by Jesus. Give Him everything you have. When you do, He will work in your life in a way that will take your breath away. With Jesus, we are never alone, and we always, *always* have help.

Do you find yourself wondering how you can believe in Jesus and allow Him to work in your life in these ways? Trusting in Jesus Christ as your Lord and Savior and acknowledging Him as the Lord of your life is as easy as ABC:

- Admit to God you're a sinner: "For all have sinned and fall short of the glory of God" (Romans 3:23).

- Believe that Jesus is God's Son: "For God so loved the world that he gave his one and only Son, that whoever believes in him shall not perish but have eternal life" (John 3:16).

- Confess your faith in Jesus as your Lord and Savior: "If you declare with your mouth, 'Jesus is Lord,' and believe in your heart that God raised him from the dead, you will be saved" (Romans 10:9).

Here's a simple prayer from the Reverend Billy Graham that you can pray today to invite Jesus into your heart and move forward in a relationship with Him:

> Dear Lord Jesus, I know that I am a sinner, and I ask for Your forgiveness. I believe You died for my sins and rose from the dead. I turn from my sins and invite You to come into my heart and life. I want to trust and follow You as my Lord and Savior. In Your Name. Amen.

If you prayed that prayer, we would love to be the first to welcome you into the family of God! As you read through the rest of this book, pray and ask the Lord to help you learn how to live your new life with Christ. Be sure to tell your minister or a Christian friend about the good news of what God has done in your life. They will be so happy for you!

Blessings to you, mama!

You Belong Here: Welcome to the Club

DEB WEAKLY

f you were here with me right now, I'd pour you a hot cup of tea and tell you three simple words: You belong here.

I've been thinking about you a lot, dear friend—or may I call you "dear sister"? I've been praying that God will speak to your heart as you read this book. I wish you could come over to my house so we could sit in my two comfy chairs and visit and talk heart to heart about the important job that you are doing with your children, whether you work a job to help support your family or stay at home full-time with your kids. Your work in your home is so important, and we're here to meet you where you are to encourage you in your calling as a mom and point you to Jesus as the source of everything you may need.

My prayer for you is that you will look at this book in your hands as a tool and as a warm hug from me and my friends here at the Help Club for Moms. This book comes with a community of like-minded women whose sole desire is to help you know the love of Jesus Christ on a new level—a personal one that is also practical—and become the woman, wife, and mother you were created to be.

As we walk through this book together, you will learn how to cultivate a soul filled with God's love. You will have a new understanding of how to apply Scripture to your everyday life.

Together, we will learn how to love our husbands and children well, with wisdom and in the power of the Holy Spirit. You may be married or in a season of singleness. You may feel battered and bruised by the scars of divorce or the rejection from the father of your child who chose not to take your hand in marriage. Or maybe this is your second marriage, and you now have a new role—stepmom—and feel terrified about the prospect of helping raise a child you haven't known all your life.

It matters not where you are in your life right now—whether married, divorced, single, or remarried. We are all in this together—with God. With the Holy Spirit's help, we will prayerfully guide you as you create a Christ-centered home—one that your kids will look back on with fondness as adults. And we will encourage you to cultivate friendships that will last a lifetime.

Our band of sisters wants to come alongside you and encourage you every step of the way in your journey as a mom. We would love for you to join our online community on Facebook or Instagram so that we can have a place to dialogue together and keep this conversation going.

We know you're short on time, so we wrote each article with you in mind. To get the most from this book, take it in snippets and apply one idea that you've learned from the reading for that day. This book is full of practical ideas, simple recipes, and fun, meaningful activities, which are found at the end of each article and designed to be lived out in your home. They emphasize one aspect of the article that we highlight to encourage your thoughts further. Then, at the end of each part, we have a beautiful list of Scriptures to encourage you in your walk with the Lord. In the back of the book, you will find our HELPful Resources, filled to the brim with practical ideas, recipes, and fun, meaningful activities for you to do with your kids.

You can use this book in your devotional time, or maybe you'll want to grab an extra copy to keep in your car so you can pick it up as you sit in the carpool line or during your kids' music lessons, sports practices, or doctor appointments.

Read the book when you can—just remember to always start with prayer, asking God to speak to your heart. Ask Him to give you something practical to take away and apply to your life each time you read.

We would *love* to bless you by giving you several exclusive *free* printables and bonus content. Thank you so much for supporting Help Club for Moms; we are so very blessed by you! Check out **myhelpclubformoms.com** and enter the code **thanks4moms** to access your free bonus resources.

Part 1

The Wise Woman Cultivates Her Spirit

Dear sister, I don't have to tell you that being a mom is exhausting. You are constantly giving and giving out to your family. You change diapers, wipe noses, break up sibling squabbles, cook a thousand meals, drive the kids everywhere, and—oh, my goodness—clean the messes. Something always needs cleaning! I remember being so tired when my kids were little that I couldn't wait until bedtime so I could crawl into my cool sheets and lay my head on my comfy pillow.

During one particularly busy season, I lamented to an older mom friend about how tired I felt and how I had nothing left to give to my husband in the evening. She said something that I will never forget: "Deb, you can't give from an empty well. You have to fill up with Jesus before you can give out to anyone else." When we fill up with Jesus each day, the Holy Spirit energizes us and gives us what we need to love and care for our families.

The Help Club for Moms loves encouraging moms to know Jesus better, so we wrote the following easy-to-read but thought-provoking articles. They are written by ordinary moms and designed to help you learn to fill up with Jesus each day so you can give out to the precious ones in your life.

love, Deb

Wave the White Flag

DEB WEAKLY

I am the vine; you are the branches. If you remain in me and I in you, you will bear much fruit; apart from me you can do nothing.

John 15:5

A Bible that is falling apart usually belongs to someone who isn't.

Charles H. Spurgeon

My daughter was four years old and my son was one. It had been another hard day. I felt overwhelmed. I lost my temper, and once again I knew I had failed. Even though I woke up with good intentions each day, desperately wanting to be a strong Christian mom, I didn't know what I was doing or what I should change. I knew I had fallen short in one way or another. This went on for a while, until finally I came to that place you might have come to before—I was at the end of myself. I began to kneel beside my daughter's bed each night after she had gone to sleep. Through tears, I prayed over her, crying out to God for help because I realized I could not be a good mom on my own.

Like a weary soldier, I waved my white flag and surrendered my fears, anxieties, and mistakes to God. Each night I repeated the phrases that weighed most heavily on my heart: "I feel lost. I don't know what I'm doing. Help me, Lord." Our good and faithful God answered me and spoke these simple words to my heart: "Deb, spend time with Me."

And so I did. I began arising fifteen to thirty minutes before my kids to meet with God: to pray, read my Bible, and journal. I always asked God for my marching orders and for wisdom to know what to do with my kids each day.

Even as I write this book, I'm reminded of all the times I went to Him over and over asking for help and wisdom, and how He answered me so faithfully. At the end of each quiet time, I wrote down what God spoke to my heart as I read the Bible and prayed. I probably have twenty-five journals, filled with prayers for myself, my kids, my husband, and our home. It's sweet to look back on the various stages of life that we experienced as a family and see God's faithfulness covering it all.

One of my favorite verses during this season was John 15:5. It says, "I am the vine; you are the branches. If you remain in me and I in you, you will bear much fruit; apart from me you can do nothing." What a beautiful promise straight from Jesus to those who choose to follow Him. We are not alone! In fact, He says that we can do nothing good or bear fruit apart from Him. We can't raise children up to know Jesus, have a successful Christian marriage, or do *anything* apart from Him. Reading this verse brought me peace and allowed me to simply come to God each day for my daily bread.

Sister, it takes humility to surrender your life and come to Jesus, not trying to do anything on your own, but I can assure you that this is the way we were meant to live in relationship with Him—in daily fellowship, coming into His presence and seeking Him through the Bible and talking with Him through prayer as we would talk to our very best friend. Jesus is a friend like no other. He knows you, your children, your husband, and your circumstances better than anyone else. He has access to your family's hearts and can help you understand how to love them well. He wants you to do as I did and wave your white flag and surrender all your cares and concerns to Him. Jesus doesn't want you to be a wife, mom, daughter, or friend on your own. He wants you to let Him into your life, your pain, your fears, and your struggles so He can make beauty from the ashes of your life and bring healing to your hurting heart.

FAITH-FILLED IDEA:
Establish the Habit of a Daily Quiet Time

If we were together in person and I was able to be completely honest with you, I would say that getting into the habit of spending regular time with God is *hard* because you are such a busy mom. But I would also say that having time with God is *crucial*—especially since you are a busy mom. If you have trouble finding time to spend with the Lord, pray and ask Him to help you get started. Here's my schedule from when my kids were little. This may be good for you, or you might want your time with God to look differently. Remember, you do you!

Twenty Minutes a Day to a Christ-Centered Home

- *Five minutes for prayer*: Commit your day to God. Ask for wisdom and help from Him.

- *Ten minutes of Bible reading*: Jot down a verse that stands out to you in your journal.

- *Five minutes to plan your day*: Write out the six most important things you need to accomplish that day, and cross them off as you complete them.

2

Let God Lead You

· · · · · · · · · · · · · DEB WEAKLY · · · · · · · · · · · · ·

*I will lead the blind by ways they have not
known, along unfamiliar paths I will guide them;
I will turn the darkness into light before them
and make the rough places smooth. These are
the things I will do; I will not forsake them.*

Isaiah 42:16

*Be assured, if you walk with Him and look to Him,
and expect help from Him, He will never fail you.*

George Müller

When my kids were growing up, I felt like a little lost puppy as I went from house to house, looking for answers on how to have a Christian home. I desperately wanted to figure out what I should be doing with my kids, so I observed the other moms that I knew. I looked over the books they had on their shelves, asked what activities they had their kids in, and took note of how they did things in their homes. I never felt like my family had it together as much as the other mothers' families did. Deep down, I knew it was dangerous to compare, as it made me feel like a failure as a mom and that my kids always fell short, but I couldn't stop noticing how confident these women were! I was so desperate to know what other people were doing in their homes because I felt like I didn't know what I was doing. I didn't want to mess up my kids or give them a childhood like the one I had, which was sad and disappointing. Because my childhood was so dysfunctional, I made lots of mistakes before I came to Jesus, and I worried that my kids would somehow do the same.

I remember one time when I felt so discouraged that I just couldn't sleep. I went downstairs in the middle of the night and broke down and cried out my heart to God because I felt like I was just not doing this "mom thing" right. I was so scared that I was going to ruin my kids and cause them to turn away from God. This scary thought made me feel debilitated and hopeless.

As I sat that night crying, I saw my Bible sitting on the table next to my chair and decided to read a few Scriptures to encourage myself. I opened to the book of Isaiah and thumbed through chapter 42 and came to verse 16 (the key at the beginning of this article). I was amazed as I read the words; they immediately went deep into my heart. There was my encouragement!

Did I feel blind and was I venturing out into unknown territory? You betcha! But through these verses, God told me He saw me and He knew I felt lost and alone. And most of all, He told me again that He would help me become the mom He created me to be. Even though I had no Christian upbringing, and in spite of my many mistakes, He said He would help me, and He encouraged me to just keep trusting Him and letting Him lead me. Knowing God met me where I was caused me to feel at peace and enabled me to keep going. He knew what my kids needed, so I needed to filter all those ideas I was seeing through Him by praying and asking.

This is a picture of the practical way we walk with Jesus and how we raise our kids with Him, one day at a time. As you read this book, get into the habit of asking the Holy Spirit to speak to you as you first crack open the pages. You will be amazed at how much you will learn if you involve God in your reading right here, right now. The Bible says that as believers, we have the Holy Spirit living inside of us, and He teaches us all the time—all we have to do is ask. Yes, we will still make mistakes because we are human, but your life will be so much better because you walked each day with Jesus.

FAITH-FILLED IDEA: Pray to Know God Better

For years I have prayed Ephesians 1:17-19 out loud to myself. These powerful Scriptures talk about the fact that we have immense power living inside of us as Christians, but we have to *pray and keep praying* to even understand it. We even have to *pray* to understand God better! It takes a spirit of wisdom and revelation.

> I keep asking that the God of our Lord Jesus Christ, the glorious Father, may give you the Spirit of wisdom and revelation, so that you may know him better. I pray that the eyes of your heart may be enlightened in order that you may know the hope to which he has called you, the riches of his glorious inheritance in his holy people, and his incomparably great power for us who believe (Ephesians 1:17-19).

3

Keep Going, Mama

························· MARI JO MAST ·························

The King will reply, "Truly I tell you, whatever you did for one of the least of these brothers and sisters of mine, you did for me."

Matthew 25:40

Trying to do the Lord's work in your own strength is the most confusing, exhausting, and tedious of all work. But when you are filled with the Holy Spirit, then the ministry of Jesus just flows out of you.

Corrie Ten Boom

I often find myself reminiscing about my early mothering years; the difficulty took me by surprise! I regularly told my husband how discouraged and hopeless I felt. Many times I would say "I'm not cut out for this" or "I cannot do this one more day." Parenting was grueling—a constant giving and serving without ever being served. On top of that, exhaustion plagued my body because my hormones were out of whack. For more than two years, I frequently struggled with panic attacks that woke and terrorized me during the night.

During this season, it seemed everything I created or crafted was either eaten, messed up, or destroyed daily. By the end of the day, I felt I literally could not make one more meal, wash one more dish, speak one more kind word, teach one more lesson, pick up one more toy, solve one more dispute, kiss one more soft cheek, or read one more Bible story.

Hopelessness became the catalyst for God to do a deep work inside of me. From the core of my heart, I prayed for the Holy Spirit to give strength, to teach, and to help, because every single day felt exhausting with no hope of change in sight. This heart cry went on for years. I actually envied my husband, who went to work and came home with a paycheck. At least at the end of the day, whatever he constructed stayed beautiful, untouched, and appreciated. Ha!

Do you feel the same?

Mama, I want you to know, the Holy Spirit taught me and stayed close this whole grueling season, even when I did not deserve it or could not feel Him. Though I'm *still* not at the finish line (the endless giving will truly never be over for us moms), I've realized our children grow, the demands ease up over time, and you forget the hardship more and more. If you are currently in a similar stage of mothering, please believe me: The raw feelings of discouragement and hopelessness eventually soften because you grow. Life's constant ebb and flow of seasons becomes more constant when we trust God. The Holy Spirit teaches us what we need to know if we ask and stay patient believing He's there. Nothing pleases Him more than when we activate our faith in Him. He heals more fully than we think possible as we continually invite Him into our mess. Today I have older, married kids who are my best friends. They thank, serve, and give back, even though ten years ago this seemed impossible.

Discouraged, weary mom, please know that every cup of cold water given in the name of Jesus brings reward. You wash the feet of Jesus when you serve and minister to your children. God sees and notices, even when no one else does. Keep serving, keep obeying God, and keep pouring out love, no matter how you feel.

If you're like me, you might be afraid of not finishing well and messing up your kids. And you know what? We *do* mess up! However, we also know staying down and defeated isn't an option. We get back up after we fall down because the Holy Spirit meets us where we are in all our worries, failures, and sins. He's so good at forgiving and pouring out His tender mercies on us every single day. God gave us His Spirit for this very reason—to help us navigate through life's journey! So take courage and try to keep the end goal in mind: What do you want your children to value and remember when they grow up?

Above all, think about this: God forgave your past, He stays active in your present, and He will help you finish strong in your future. I'm so glad He never, ever leaves us! Do not be weary in well-doing, but keep on blazing a faithful trail and stay close to Him. Your beautiful rewards are on the way—they are coming soon. When you see the eternal investment you've made in your children, you will be pleasantly surprised and blown away by the goodness of God!

FAITH-FILLED IDEA:
Use Your Imagination in Prayer

God gave us an imagination to draw us closer to Him—it's a powerful tool we can utilize to connect our spirit with His Spirit. Close your eyes and imagine yourself standing in front of Jesus at the end of your life. Ask Him to speak to you. Take a notebook or journal and write down the important things He relays to you. Ask Him to help you live out daily what He says. Make a few copies of your notes and place them in strategic places in your home where you can be reminded of them daily.

4

Making Room for Prayer

RAE-ELLEN SANDERS

*When you pray, go into your room, close
the door and pray to your Father, who is
unseen. Then your Father, who sees what
is done in secret, will reward you.*

Matthew 6:6

*Satan trembles when he sees the
weakest Christian on his knees.*

William Cowper

love the movie *War Room*. The little old woman, Clara, is a power-house prayer warrior! She diligently removes herself to a tiny room where she has lined the walls with pictures and Scriptures to motivate her in her spiritual battle through prayer. The movie inspires me to fight the enemy with the Word of God and to persevere when my prayers aren't answered in my timing. According to James 5:16 (NKJV), "The effective, fervent prayer of a righteous man avails much." From what I understand about Scripture, the most spiritually successful people were men and women of prayer. Jesus Himself constantly removed himself from the crowds to find quiet time with the Father. If Jesus, as our greatest example, found time to pray, how much more should we follow His standard to pray!

Creating a secret place to meet the Lord in prayer is how we begin to make quiet time a life-changing priority. A comfy chair or a nook reserved for your prayer closet or war room will allow you to slow down, quiet your heart, read God's Word without interruption, hear the voice of the Lord, and pray. First, find a simple space. If you have a spare bedroom, office, or closet, use it! Tidy it and remove anything that will cause a distraction so you will be able to meditate on God, the things of God, and the work of God. You can use a chair, kneel on a comfy mat or pillow, or lie before the Lord. You will need ample wall space for Scripture, prayer reminders, clippings, and photos. You may need a lamp, depending on the location, and a Bible, pen, journal, hymnal, or music player.

If you're like me and don't have room in your house for a dedicated war room, another option would be to create a prayer board made from a trifold board that you can find at most office stores. I've added prayer cues and Scriptures to my board that move me to pray. Pinterest has been a great resource to help me tailor my board to my liking. Turn to page 181 to learn how to make a prayer board.

When opened, my board shields me from the laundry and other distractions that want to pull me away from time with God. When I am finished, it folds up and easily stores under my bed. After creating this safe haven and refuge from the world, go into your "secret place" and thank God for all His blessings and provisions. Thanksgiving gives you a humble posture for prayer. You can journal your praises and even acknowledge answered prayers. Play music that inspires to you sing songs of praise. Pick up a hymnal or sing songs you know from church. Psalm 22:3 (NLT) states, "Yet you are holy, enthroned on the praises of Israel." Lifting your voice in worship invites the Lord to join you. Open your Bible, and before reading, ask the Holy Spirit to give you wisdom to understand the mysteries of His Word. Read Scripture out loud. Take notes, underline, and meditate on what the Lord has spoken to you. If you feel like trying something new, sing the words like David did in the Psalms. Don't forget to be specific in this time of conversing with God and pray for people by name. Your quiet time will become a time of refreshment with the Lord that might even become your favorite part of the day!

FAITH-FILLED IDEA:
Help Your Kids Spend Time with Jesus

Model this daily quiet time and teach your kids the value of spending time with Jesus. When your children see you in your prayer closet, they will know it is your secret time with Jesus and won't interrupt (as much). Help them find a cozy corner dedicated to spending time with God for themselves, equipped with a children's Bible, a snack, *Wee Sing Bible Songs*, a journal, and a pencil. You could even help them make their own prayer board. Prayer is the most important thing we can do for our children! It will impact them when we are gone. May the Lord bless you as you seek Him in your silent retreat from the world. Be ready to see breakthroughs in your war room!

5

Your Prayers Outlive Your Life!

···················· DEB WEAKLY ····················

My prayer is not for them alone. I pray also for those who will believe in me through their message, that all of them may be one, Father, just as you are in me and I am in you. May they also be in us so that the world may believe that you have sent me.

John 17:20-21

Prayers are deathless. They outlive the lives of those who uttered them.

E.M. Bounds

struggled with my weight as a teenager. Over time, I decided to slowly start exercising. This simple habit helped me want to eat a little better and maintain a healthier body weight. But then we had kids, and I found out how hard it was to maintain a habit of exercise as a new mom! Getting the kids out the door to the gym was impossible, so we purchased a cheap treadmill. I decided I could get my workout in first thing in the morning before the kids got up. At the beginning, running on the treadmill was great, but then I began to get bored. It became harder and harder to motivate myself to get up and run.

During this season, I discovered what is now one of my favorite movies, *The Gospel of John*. I began watching it as I ran, and this routine not only kept me exercising, but God used those little treadmill sessions to change my life. In the movie, the characters only speak word-for-word Scripture, so it helped me understand Jesus better by allowing me to visualize what was happening in the book of John and how Jesus lived His life on the earth. I was hooked on this video and couldn't get enough of it! Since I didn't go to church as a kid, I had no idea who Jesus was. God really used this workout time to help me grow in intimacy with Jesus.

I love the scene in the movie where Jesus prayed for His disciples and for all the believers who were to become Christians from their message. As I watched, I began to realize that Jesus was praying for me and the entire body of believers to be one, as He and the Father are one. This prayer that Jesus prayed more than two thousand years ago is still being answered today and will keep being answered in the lives of other believers until He comes back to the earth. I was so excited because it became clear to me that our prayers keep going too. Since God is outside of time and can answer our prayers in any moment or any year, our prayers are timeless!

Let's think about this for a second. Our prayers reach further and are more powerful than any of us could ever understand on this side of heaven. I love how E.M. Bounds, a Civil War army chaplain who was known for praying for four hours each day, put it:

> How vast are the possibilities of prayer! How wide is its reach! What great things are accomplished by this divinely appointed means of grace! It lays its hand on Almighty God and moves him to do what he would not otherwise do if prayer was not offered. It brings things to pass which would never otherwise occur. The story of prayer is the story of great achievements. Prayer is a wonderful power placed by Almighty God in the hands of his saints, which may be used to accomplish great purposes and to achieve unusual results. Prayer reaches to everything, takes in all things great and small which are promised by God to the children of men. The only limit to prayer are the promises of God and his ability to fulfill those promises. "Open thy mouth wide and I will fill it."[1]

E.M. Bounds had a great understanding of the power of prayer. Our prayers move heaven and achieve unusual results. I love the fact that our prayers are timeless. When we pray, we are sending a message forward to a time we will not see! Our prayers transcend time and keep going, even for our great-great-grandchildren and beyond. Think about it: We can pray now for those in our lineage to know Christ and to serve Him with their whole heart. This is really good news, especially if you're like me and weren't raised in a Christian home, because you can pray and have a completely different family lineage. God makes *all* the difference in our lives and brings lasting change. So take the box off of God and pray big prayers!

FAITH-FILLED IDEA: Make a Prayer Binder

My prayer binder has meant the world to me over the years, and I still refer to it often. It's a great place to keep the prayers you want to pray regularly over your family at your fingertips. On page 182, you will find everything you need to help you get started. You can also go to https://helpclubformoms.com/how -to-make-a-prayer-binder/ for more detailed instructions and examples of my personal prayers for my husband and kids from years ago. Making a prayer binder and praying for your family regularly is worth the time and effort, and it will change your life and the life of your family.

6

Replacing Lies with Truth

····················· KRISTALL WILLIS ·····················

*Summing it all up, friends, I'd say you'll do best
by filling your minds and meditating on things
true, noble, reputable, authentic, compelling,
gracious—the best, not the worst; the beautiful, not
the ugly; things to praise, not things to curse. Put
into practice what you learned from me, what
you heard and saw and realized. Do that, and
God, who makes everything work together, will
work you into his most excellent harmonies.*

Philippians 4:8-9 MSG

*The battle you wage against your human nature is an
invisible one that will be won or lost in the mind. Minute
by minute, hour by hour, in the hidden workshop of
your mind, you are constructing thoughts of good
or evil, depression or joy, success or failure. You are
writing your own life story as a human being with
each subtle and soundless thought you think.*

Tommy Newberry, *The 4:8 Principle*

'm a bad mom."

"I'm not successful or productive."

"I can't do this."

These are the words I hear sometimes in my mind. Do you hear them too?

Quite often, I struggle with toxic thoughts about myself that cause me to respond to my kids out of frustration and irritation. I lose my patience with them when they are just simply being kids, and then I feel worse. My children suffer and are not seeing the best version of me as a mommy because I am believing *lies*! Why do we believe these lies about ourselves? The truth is that the enemy of our souls wants to plant this constant negative thought chatter in our minds. Satan is crafty and manipulative, and he relishes in our weakness. But guess what, mama? Jesus is stronger, and His authority will triumph in our mothering!

In trying to stop this cycle, I have turned to Scripture to find the truth. The Word of God is filled with so much encouragement, strength, and power. Proverbs 15:1 says, "A gentle answer turns away wrath, but a harsh word stirs up anger," and James 1:19 says, "Be quick to listen, slow to speak and slow to become angry." These Scriptures have become unwavering truths for me and are now in my arsenal to wield against Satan.

I have found the practice of turning my worries and fears into prayers also helps exchange these lies with truths. For example, when I worry about my children getting hurt, I'll say, "Lord, please protect and watch over them. Send Your angels to guard and guide them." Or when I worry about my husband, I'll pray, "Lord, be with my husband as he works. Give him confidence in You to follow Your will and feel Your Spirit's presence around him. Strengthen him to rely on You and show him You are his provider and how much You love him." This takes control from the enemy and passes my burdens over to our Lord and Savior (Psalm 55:22; Matthew 11:28-30).

Our "enemy the devil prowls around like a roaring lion looking for someone to devour" (1 Peter 5:8). The devil is ready and waiting to tempt you and bring you down that rabbit hole of bad thoughts again and again! Remember, though, he is not very creative and tends to use the same triggers over and over. He will also plant thoughts in your own mind, in first-person, trying to make you think it is actually your own thoughts. What a lie indeed. *Any thought we have that doesn't line up with the Word is from Satan.* We have to constantly remember the Word of God and hide it deep in our hearts (Deuteronomy 6:6-8).

God knew in our humanness that we would struggle with our thoughts. He gave us many Scriptures to help us battle them—we are not meant to fight this battle alone! Here are five key verses that speak directly to our minds and thought life:

- "Be transformed by the renewing of your mind" (Romans 12:2).

- "Take captive every thought to make it obedient to Christ" (2 Corinthians 10:5).

- "Be made new in the attitude of your minds" (Ephesians 4:23).

- "Let this mind be in you which was also in Christ Jesus" (Philippians 2:5 NKJV).

- "Set your minds on things above, not on earthly things" (Colossians 3:2).

This practice of fixing our minds on things from above is not something we tend to do naturally—it takes prayer, discipline, obedience, and continued practice. By filling our mind with God's Word we can begin responding with truth from Scripture. Oh, how this will change our daily interactions, responses, and moods!

FAITH-FILLED IDEA: Replace Lies with Truth

What lies are you believing? A great way to redirect our thoughts is to find Scriptures that negate the negative ones. Keep these verses in places you'll see often and reflect on them so they become ingrained in your mind. Reference the chart on page 183 in the "HELPful Resources" section, and then write your own "Replacing Lies with Truth" chart. Go through this exercise while prayerfully asking God to reveal His truth to you.

Also, please visit joychallengeformoms.com, where you can take "The 40-Day Joy Challenge for Moms." This is a simple and fun online program based on God's Word that helps produce better habits, stronger relationships, and greater joy in less than nine minutes per day.

7

God's love Brings Freedom

RACHEL JONES

*I have loved you with a love that lasts forever. I have
kept on loving you with a kindness that never fails.*

Jeremiah 31:3 NIRV

*It's not about finding ways to avoid God's judgment
and feeling like a failure if you don't do everything
perfectly. It's about fully experiencing God's love and
letting it perfect you. It's not about being somebody
you are not. It's about becoming who you really are.*

Stormie Omartian

My husband and I recently attended a charity ball. It was an
incredible experience. The theme of the night was that God's
love brings freedom and ultimately wins every battle. After
all, nothing is stronger and more resilient than God's love. As I sat in
the audience and listened to the speakers that evening, I trembled and
felt incredibly amazed by God's love, and His presence filled me with
awe! I was reminded that our past will never define us and that God
has already rewritten our story. One of my favorite verses in the Bible
confirms this:

> Nothing can ever separate us from God's love. Neither
> death nor life, neither angels nor demons, neither our fears
> for today nor our worries about tomorrow—not even the
> powers of hell can separate us from God's love (Romans
> 8:38 NLT).

This love cannot be vanquished, and it is relentless, pursuing us even in our sinful state. But if we don't understand the Lord's love—if we pull away from Him due to guilt, anxiety, or fear or if we are not walking in His complete freedom—we aren't living up to our full potential.

As I sat and listened to one of the speakers at the ball share her story, I was fully aware of God's power. This woman revealed how for years she felt something missing in her life. She admitted that due to shame from an abortion and a divorce, her inability to fully accept God's love was hindering her as a mother and as a wife to her new husband.

She went on to powerfully proclaim Jesus Christ and His authority. She shared that one day, He spoke to her, and her life was radically changed. God's love changed her life, as it did mine, and it can change yours too. The love and grace of Jesus Christ are so completely freeing because they lead us to true worship, as we are forever grateful for His undeserved love. We are then focused on Him, not on our failings. Let me say that again: We are *not* focused on our failings! We have a calling higher than ourselves and an inheritance that is unfading—entirely built on His perfect love.

Because of Christ's love, we have all been redeemed from something weak to something wonderful! He is worthy, and He clothes us in His perfect worthiness when we accept Him and become His daughters. Dear mama, after we have become one with Him and He fills us with His Spirit, *He* brings complete freedom from our past, who we were, into our lives. "For the Lord is the Spirit, and wherever the Spirit of the Lord is, there is freedom" (2 Corinthians 3:17 NLT). Freedom is powerful. It is a gift and a treasure to be freed from condemnation!

We also have the Almighty on our side fighting for us. As we battle daily with guilt and worry, He is there, offering His unconditional love.

> "Because he loves me," says the LORD, "I will rescue him; I will protect him, for he acknowledges my name. He will call upon me, and I will answer him; I will be with him in trouble, I will deliver him and honor him" (Psalm 91:14-15).

The heart of our Father is revealed in these two verses from Psalms.

Nothing can penetrate the protective shield and the freedom that God has placed around our spirits. When we trust that we are eternally secure because of God's great love and His ultimate triumph over evil, we can experience an unwavering serenity that transcends our circumstances.

I now live with more confidence and certainty because of promises that I have received from the Lord. I regularly pray for clarity regarding my path and my purpose for being on this earth. He has guided me to fiercely love the people He has put in front of me (especially my husband and kids) and to loudly proclaim what a life as a Christian woman looks like in our culture. But this is not my nature. I am a very selfish person, and I have so many memories of ignoring those close to me and saying things that hurt them. I enjoy being admired—I mean, who doesn't? I would not be proud of the woman I am if it weren't for Jesus (perhaps you can relate). He has changed my heart and given me a supernatural love for people. He has helped me walk in freedom, not caring what others think and not needing others' approval.

FAITH-FILLED IDEA: "Redeemed"

Pick a night this week, or even thirty minutes over the weekend, to be alone. Ask your sweet husband to watch the kids and allow yourself this time. Listen to the Big Daddy Weave song "Redeemed."

If this song touches you as it has me, share it with that sweet husband of yours. Talk together about the "heavy chains" that you need to shake off. Grow together as a couple in the complete freedom of Christ.

8

Never Gonna Stop Singing

······· RAE-ELLEN SANDERS ·······

*Jehoshaphat bowed down with his face to the
ground, and all the people of Judah and Jerusalem
fell down in worship before the Lord...After consulting
the people, Jehoshaphat appointed men to sing
to the Lord and to praise him for the splendor of
his holiness as they went out at the head of the
army, saying: "Give thanks to the Lord, for his
love endures forever." As they began to sing and
praise, the Lord set ambushes against the men
of Ammon and Moab and Mount Seir who were
invading Judah, and they were defeated.*

2 Chronicles 20:18,21-22

*We need to discover all over again that worship
is natural to the Christian, as it was to the godly
Israelites who wrote the psalms, and that the habit of
celebrating the greatness and graciousness of God
yields an endless flow of thankfulness, joy, and zeal.*

J.I. Packer

Picture a woman on her knees with tears streaming down her
face. Worshippers singing to the Lord surround her, their
hands raised in abandon of the world and naysayers. She
kneels without consideration of others and feels the presence of God
all around her like a blanket.

I had this spiritual revelation as I sat in church recently, broken and
deflated by the worries of the world. That Sunday, I was transformed

by the renewing of my mind through song. Yep, you read that right. Singing and bowing in reverence unlocked my burden! Just like King Jehoshaphat in today's Scripture reading, praising the Lord defeated my worry. While the Israelites praised the Lord with singing, God did the fighting for them. The King of Judah took his faith in God and his worship seriously, and the results were miraculous!

Have you ever left church feeling lighter than before you entered because of genuine worship? Collective and personal worship might not change your situation, but it can change your perspective like it did mine. I still went home to face my trials, but I encountered Jesus in the throne room and danced with the lover of my soul. In exchange for my adoration, He gave me His peace. I felt that my deepest thoughts were known and that I was accepted anyway. It was like reaching into the spiritual realm where God communicates with our spirit or soul and receiving a big hug from Abba—our Daddy!

God's principles never change—He will fight for you if you spend your life singing and praising the Lord. In fact, worship is so powerful that it is an actual weapon against the enemy! "The weapons we fight with are not the weapons of the world. On the contrary, they have divine power to demolish strongholds" (2 Corinthians 10:4). Sister, when you face an enemy who is coming against your life—marriage, parenting, finances, or health—you might want to do what an earthly king did…fall on your face in worship. If it was good enough for King Jehoshaphat and King David, it is definitely good enough for you and me!

When we seek the Lord wholeheartedly, nothing else matters. Praise is driven not by our emotions nor by what others think about us nor even by our performance, but by our will to be in the presence of the Father. It isn't the song or the leader; it's our souls connecting with heaven. However, songs are imperative to help us enter His gates with thanksgiving and His courts with praise (Psalm 100:4). God doesn't care if we sing on key; He simply cares that we *sing*! It is not the song that is important to God, but the heart of the worshipper. In fact, the times we don't feel like praising God are the very moments that we should. When we acknowledge God as Almighty and desire Him over everything else, we are essentially fueled to worship. Whether it is sing-ing, reverently lying before the Lord, or jumping up and dancing, our problems don't have anything against the power of praise!

We are to praise God in *all* situations—when we are on top of the world and when we are beaten down and defeated, when we are in lack and when we have plenty. The next time you feel discouraged or defeated, start praising the Lord. When your children are having a meltdown or your marriage is shaky, praise the Lord! When you choose to break out in worship during the most crucial times in your life, you might just be set free from the circumstances that bind you. Sister, it's time to get your song back! Don't allow the enemy to mute you—use the weapon of worship and never stop singing.

FAITH-FILLED IDEA: Worship

Worship at home and make it a daily routine! Find praise music that lifts your heart and soul, and play it often. Encourage your family to dance and worship with you. Even your husband will feel his burdens lift as he dances around the living room. If he thinks it's not manly, remind him that King David danced!

9

Finding Faith in the Pit

KRISTALL WILLIS

I pray that God, the source of hope, will fill you completely with joy and peace because you trust in him. Then you will overflow with confident hope through the power of the Holy Spirit.

Romans 15:13 NLT

God delights to increase the faith of His children. We ought, instead of wanting no trials before victory, no exercise for patience, to be willing to take them from God's hands as a means. Trials, obstacles, difficulties and sometimes defeats, are the very food of faith.

George Müller

About a year ago, I received a phone call from my husband, who said the dreaded words no wife wants to hear: "I lost my job today." My heart sank, and my mouth became so dry I was unable to speak. We were in a deep, dark pit, and all I wanted was for us to be out of this stressful time and back in our comfortable ways.

Losing a job is tough. It affects our husbands more than we can ever understand. They lose a sense of their identity and feel helpless. It was a very low time in my life and my marriage. Maybe you have been there or are living this life right now, and we had been there before. But this time, we knew God had a path for us. Rather than trying to solve the dilemma as quickly as possible and jump into a new job as fast as we could, putting a Band-Aid on our problem, we approached it differently than before—we prayed big-time! We took an inward look at our sinful lives and really did some soul-searching. We went through a "pruning" period, which was extremely hard, but as any gardener knows, after a good pruning, the next harvest produces plenty of good fruit (John 15).

While in that season, the Lord called me to His Word and filled me with hope. The hope I felt was not just a hollow desire, wishing for a good or a quick outcome. Instead, it was a deep certainty, rooted in the depth of our souls and shrouded in "confident expectation."[2] I have learned that this kind of hope gives us a confidence that no earthly definition of hope can reach (Romans 15:13 NLT). As I began to read my Bible daily, I was reminded to *persevere* (Romans 5:3-5; Hebrews 10:36; James 1:2-12), find new *confidence* to walk in God's ways (Romans 12:12; 15:13 NLT; Ephesians 3:12; Hebrews 10:35), and discover a renewed *trust* to rely on Him (Proverbs 3:5-6; Jeremiah 17:7-8). Nowhere did I find the Bible saying we should give up, rush through our problems, or prove to the world we could survive on our own. Most important, I didn't find verses saying it was even possible to live a comfortable life free from hardship.

Throughout our trials, I was continually drawn to Hebrews 10:19–12:3. These chapters talk about suffering, holding onto our promises, and the ancient people who were known for their great faith. Many of them suffered deeply and did not even receive their promises, yet still they were living by faith when they died (Hebrews 11:13,39). By choosing to activate their faith, they walked in obedience, trusting God would lead them. I believe God was leading my husband and me to a new place too, and this place would be rooted in Him and prepared in advance, just like the Israelites (Exodus 23:20-23). We also quickly began to realize that our obedience and discipline were of utmost importance to our Father (Hebrews 12:7-11). Now we start every weekday praying together while he drives to work, and we check in to see how the other is doing—if we're still walking in God's will for us, leaving our old habits behind. We support each other by standing firm together and keeping each other accountable!

Whatever pit you may be in right now, do not give up. Instead, seek

God's path for you—ask Him to lead you—and allow yourself to *trust* Him. The truth that He is always with us and goes before us makes breaking out of the pit possible! Release the grip on your fears and anxieties and let God direct you (Matthew 11:28-30). Don't be grabbing those burdens back either, acting like you know best, but rather trust His process for your own growth. Our faith isn't something that is always recognizable or measurable, but know that God sees our faith. He goes ahead of us and prepares a way, a home in His kingdom, just as He led our ancestors to victory! Sister, let's build our faith by walking in confident hope—knowing that through our trust in God, He will be faithful in all situations and scenarios we face.

FAITH-FILLED IDEA: A Statement of Faith

Write your own "by faith" statement about yourself. Reflect on your life and think about how God would describe your walk of faith. When have you responded purely out of faithfulness and obedience to Him? Reference Hebrews 11 for examples.

For example, mine would say, "By faith, Kristall, when God tested her, stood by her husband and trusted God's ways were better. She stepped aside, disregarded worldly wisdom, and trusted God to use her husband to lift their family out of the pit."

10

living by the Spirit

······· JENNIFER VALDOIS ·······

*Those who live according to the flesh have their
minds set on what the flesh desires; but those
who live in accordance with the Spirit have
their minds set on what the Spirit desires. The
mind governed by the flesh is death, but the
mind governed by the Spirit is life and peace.*

Romans 8:5-6

*O Holy Spirit, descend plentifully into my heart.
Enlighten the dark corners of this neglected
dwelling and scatter there Thy cheerful beams.*

Saint Augustine

As excited as I was to become a wife and mother, I felt utterly unprepared for the challenges that were ahead of me. When I was an overwhelmed young mom, I turned to the world for guidance. During those years, I looked for help and searched for answers about life, marriage, and parenting by watching afternoon television shows, talking with friends, and reading self-help books. As I look back, I was so hopeless during those years. The storms of life were overwhelmingly difficult to navigate, and the darkness was all-consuming. It was impossible to find my way—I needed God's Word to light my path.

Although I was a Christian and attended church every Sunday, I did not spend time in God's Word, seeking Him for leadership and direction. I needed revelation that Jesus was the Light of the World (John

8:12) and that He stepped out of heaven, took the form of man, and came to save the lost—like me (Luke 19:10). Dear mama, maybe you are like me and you need to take your relationship with God to a new level and start reading your Bible every day.

Have you ever been camping when there is a new moon? When the sun goes down, you must be ready for the darkness, carrying a flashlight to light your way. Even if you have a campfire burning or a bright lantern lit at the picnic table, you still won't be able to see the path to your campsite. Without your flashlight, you walk in the shadows and risk tripping over rocks or stumbling on uneven ground. This is the same for us when we are living in darkness. We grope our way around obstacles and occasionally stub our toes. We need the Light of the World to illuminate our way.

I love the metaphor that God's Word is our flashlight for life. Psalm 119:105 says, God's "word is a lamp for my feet, a light on my path." God's Word illuminates our path so we can see and avoid the mud and the mire of this world, otherwise known as bad choices or wrong turns. His Word will light our way, directing each and every step. When we read and meditate on Scripture, it transforms our thinking.

When you became a Christian, God gave you the Holy Spirit to come and live inside of you to help you understand the mysteries of the Bible. He teaches and reminds you what Jesus taught (John 14:26), and He guides you into all truth (John 16:13). You don't need to walk in the darkness any longer; you can use the "flashlight" of God's Word to light your way.

FAITH-FILLED IDEA: A Quiet-Time Basket

Fill a basket with all the supplies you'll need for quiet time with God. Everything will be at your fingertips every time you meet with Jesus! Here are some ideas:

your Bible	journal
highlighters or pens	chocolates

devotional books   thank-you cards

sticky notes

Need extra time to spend with the Lord? Check out our great recipe for "Easy Crockpot Taco Soup" on page 186. It's easy to throw together a quick meal in the morning so later in the day, while your children are napping or playing quietly, you can sneak away with a cup of tea and spend some time with the Lord.

Scriptures to Ponder

WHO IS HE?

He is mighty to save (Zephaniah 3:17).

He is love (1 John 4:16).

He conquers Satan, our accuser (Revelation 12:10).

He is the giver of life (Psalm 36:9).

He fights for us and gives us victory (Deuteronomy 20:4).

He cleans our hearts and makes us whole (1 John 1:9).

He is our healer (Exodus 15:26).

He is the One who sets us free (Galatians 5:1).

He is our Redeemer (Isaiah 44:22).

He is our Risen Savior (1 Timothy 1:15).

He is righteous (Zephaniah 3:5).

He makes all things new (Isaiah 43:18-19).

He is our strength (Psalm 46:1).

He is our protector (Psalm 18:2).

He is light (1 John 1:5).

He is the One who knows us and chose us (Ephesians 1:4-5).

He is gracious and merciful (Psalm 116:5).

He is our deliverer from trouble (Psalm 34:19).

He is holy (1 Samuel 2:2).

He is faithful (2 Timothy 2:13).

He is our Father (Ephesians 4:6).

He is the most gracious forgiver (Ephesians 1:7-8).

He is our perfect peace (Ephesians 2:14-18).

He is the giver of all good things (James 1:17).

He began a good work in us and will complete it
(Philippians 1:6).

He is the promised Anointed One (Daniel 9:25-26).

He is the One we are called to follow (Matthew 4:19-20).

He is the One who indwells us (1 Corinthians 3:16).

WHO AM I?

I have been saved by Jesus (1 Peter 1:23).

I am loved (1 John 4:10).

I am blameless and free from accusation (Colossians 1:22).

I have life (1 John 5:12).

I am victorious through Jesus Christ (1 Corinthians 15:57).

I am clean (John 15:3).

I have been healed (Isaiah 53:5).

I am free forever from condemnation (Romans 8:1).

I have been redeemed (Revelation 5:9).

I have been saved and set apart by God (2 Timothy 1:9).

I am a slave of righteousness (Romans 6:18).

I am a new creation (2 Corinthians 5:17).

I have strength in exchange for my weakness
(2 Corinthians 12:9-10).

I am protected from the evil one (1 John 5:18).

I am a daughter of light and not of darkness
(1 Thessalonians 5:5).

I am chosen of God, holy and dearly loved (Colossians 3:12).

I find God's mercy and grace in my time of need (Hebrews 4:16).

I am more than a conqueror through Christ (Romans 8:37).

I have been sanctified and called to holiness (1 Corinthians 1:2).

I have faith (Romans 12:3).

I am a child of God (John 1:12).

I am forgiven on the account of Jesus's name (1 John 2:12).

I have been given peace (John 14:27).

I've been given power, love, and self-discipline (2 Timothy 1:7).

I have been made complete in Christ (Colossians 2:10).

I am anointed by God (1 John 2:27).

I am commissioned to make disciples (Matthew 28:19-20).

I have Christ in me (Colossians 1:27).

Part 2

The Wise Woman Loves Her Husband

I am so happy to say that, at the time of this writing, my husband, Randy, and I are about to celebrate our twenty-eighth year of marriage. As empty-nesters, we realize now how blessed we are to have worked at our marriage and put in the time and effort it takes to love each other well with God's help. Our marriage has had its fair share of struggles, but I can honestly say that Randy is my best friend. Ruth Bell Graham wrote this about relationships like ours: "A happy marriage is the union of two good forgivers."

Mama, the greatest gift you can give your children is to keep forgiving, choosing to love, and to stay married to their dad. We pray the following articles will encourage and also challenge you. The moms who wrote them have marriages that all have issues, but one thing we try to do is to keep coming back to God and asking Him for help. These articles don't provide ten steps to a perfect marriage, but they do wrestle with topics like pride, leadership, respect, intimacy, and companionship.

If you're a single mom, we want you to know that we absolutely love you, and we didn't leave you out of this section. We have written a message just for you called "Encouragement for Single Moms" (see page 83) that includes a powerful activity. We pray you will feel the Lord's love as you read.

love, Deb

11

The Power of Humility and a Positive Word

········· TARA DAVIS ·········

*May the words of my mouth and the
meditation of my heart be pleasing to you,
O LORD, my rock and my redeemer.*

Psalm 19:14 NLT

*Marriage is one of the most humbling, sanctifying
journeys you will ever be a part of. It forces us to
wrestle with our selfishness and pride. But it also
gives us a platform to display love and commitment.*

Francis Chan

Oh, my friend, think back to your wedding day. It was beautiful, wasn't it? The vows were said, the cake was cut, and as we crossed the threshold of married life, we were ready for our fairytale to begin. We had found our Prince Charming, and he was our absolute dream come true.

Maybe you don't remember exactly when it happened, but eventually you may have realized that in your fairytale there was no perfect glass slipper, no magical kiss to awaken all the hidden, dying parts of your heart. Perhaps you sometimes felt you were promised such beauty but unwrapped a gift of disappointment instead. Oh, how we would love to blame our husbands for these unmet expectations and unfulfilled dreams! However, the problem doesn't lie solely within the man we pledged our life to. No, sister, the problem is within you and me, and we must take it to the foot of the cross.

My friend, our expectations for our husbands and marriages are often so high that they pave the way for subtle criticism to seep into our thoughts, words, and even our prayers. This habit of criticism, though seemingly harmless, can be the destruction of our marriage. Girl, we have got to get this under control, don't we? I am right there with you, praying, "Lord, change me." And that is where it begins—submitting ourselves to our Savior and allowing Him to do a healing work in our hearts. He will show you what you need to change, just as He is showing me.

The foundation for hope within my marriage began with humility. I remember reading the story of the Pharisee and the tax collector in Luke 18:9-14, and it shattered my heart. I was the Pharisee in my marriage. I was the one who proudly looked down and declared myself beyond reproach in our relationship. What a prideful fool I had been. I needed to pray, to beat my chest before the Lord, and to ask for mercy. I asked Him to reveal my own faults and, in turn, gave the depravity of my heart back to the Lord, allowing Him to tenderly work in me.

When we see the truth about ourselves, we are able to look at our husbands through eyes of compassion instead of criticism. He caused me to see how sinful and selfish my actions and expectations were. I had placed an unnecessary burden of perfectionism on my husband.

Then the Lord so lovingly pointed out my hurtful thoughts regarding him. Those little thoughts seemed so innocent and justified, but they were hardening my heart toward him and tearing us apart. The Lord prompted me to pause immediately when a negative thought toward my husband flashed through my mind and instead replace it with a thought that gives life. This one little action, unapparent to anyone but me, changed my life. I began to see my husband in a new way. Those unmet expectations, the need for my fairytale, faded away, and I was able to see my husband through the eyes of Christ and love him just the way he is, just as Christ loves me.

Finally, the Lord prompted me to exhibit love for my husband through my words, complimenting him instead of condemning, speaking highly of him to others instead of complaining. When you do this, your husband will see the light of Christ's love shining through you! But that wasn't the end of it, even my prayers needed to change. Instead of grumbling to the Lord about my husband, He showed me how to speak prayers of blessing even when I wanted to shout words that curse. I needed to pray that my husband, through the power of the Holy Spirit, would know the vast height, depth, and love of the Lord. When you become your husband's prayer warrior, your priorities shift. You begin to delight in things of the Lord instead of the silly, girlish fairy tales you used to hold as your standard for happiness.

Your marriage doesn't have to be perfect to be beautiful, my friend. God makes beautiful things out of ashes. Give Him the ashes of your life, and let Him do His beautiful work. Shed the burdens of your unmet expectations, the shackles of your critical spirit, and pick up the power of the Holy Spirit to help you speak life through your words, to birth peace through your thoughts, and move mountains through your prayers! I pray that God will continue to change each of our hearts toward our husbands and that He will give us the humility to fall more deeply in love with our husbands every day.

FAITH-FILLED IDEA: Be Restored

Ask God today to reveal the darkest parts of your heart to you so that you can give them back to Him for restoration and forgiveness. In order to love like Jesus, you have to confront who you really are instead of simply seeing yourself the way you would like to be. God is able to heal all things, my friend, including you.

12

Kindness in Marriage

······· MARI JO MAST ·······

The Holy Spirit produces this kind of fruit in our lives: love, joy, peace, patience, kindness, goodness, faithfulness, gentleness, and self-control. There is no law against these things.

Galatians 5:22-23 NLT

He who plants kindness, gathers love.

Saint Basil

Oh, friend, I want to share something that's dear to my heart: a personal story about kindness and the big difference it made in my marriage.

Are you like me? When you think of a failing marriage, do you assume the big, obvious sins are the culprits that damage and destroy? I thought so too. Sadly, it took me a while to realize that small, subtle sins lead to larger, more noticeable ones over time—they gradually become a weapon for the enemy to wield against godly marriages if they go unchecked. Daily duties come fairly easy for me; however, doing them with a kind heart can be a bit more challenging.

My husband and I have been married for twenty-six years, and we have seven children (three are married). It's easy to take each other for granted when you've been married a long time unless you're intentional. A few years ago, I had an eye-opening conversation with my husband. It's highlighted in my memory because I learned an important lesson I don't want to forget. I experienced a difficult season in my life as a mom; I was trying so hard to stay faithful with the daily things, yet I felt I was failing. The laundry pile and the constant flow of meals to prepare for my big family overwhelmed me, and the dirty dishes and cleaning made me weary. Ministering to my children's needs was important to me, yet there were constant interruptions. Sometimes a sickness would pop up out of the blue. On one evening, I felt irritable, tired, and worn out from all of the above. I was unkind and snappy to my husband while we were having a conversation, and he grew quiet. He seemed distant and more discouraged than I had noticed before. Sadness filled his eyes, and I knew something was very wrong. I felt awful seeing him this way, and I wondered what it could be.

He said something like, "I know you have so much on your plate. You have all the children to watch over and to care for while I'm at work. Even though you have an endless amount of responsibility, can you at least be kind to me?"

My eyes opened as he spoke, and it pierced me to the heart! When had I stopped showing kindness to my best friend? Sadly, I had slipped into a pattern of self-centeredness and complaining so slowly I hadn't noticed.

This wasn't the kind of legacy I wanted to leave behind. That night, I cried out to God. I told my husband I was sorry and asked if he could forgive me. I was overwhelmed with all the responsibilities as a mom, but I didn't want to treat him that way. I realized I had been holding bitterness in my heart toward my husband. Although his plate was full too, I had been blind to it. I finally saw that we were on the same team, even though our job descriptions were very different. We both shared big challenges with our large family, but we were committed for the long haul. My marriage meant more to me than anything else, so I was willing to change my behavior.

How grateful I am that Jesus helps us when we're struggling. I don't know where I'd be without Him! He turned my unkindness around and showed me how to become more aware, more purposeful, and more intentional. Anything worth fighting for takes a team effort with Jesus. True change happens when we work together with Him. Although it took place years ago, I try to keep this incident in the forefront of my mind. Kindness became a priority because I wanted my marriage to last. I'm far from perfect, but with God's help, I'm not where I used to be. Nothing ministers to my husband like physical touch, so I've found this is a great way for me to express kindness to him. I occasionally try to look for opportunities to give him a hug or kiss when he's not expecting it. When we're alone, I sometimes initiate intimacy. Self-sacrificial kindness has so many rewards in the end. I believe kindness saved our marriage in more ways than one.

Friend, I wrote this to encourage you. I don't know what your marriage looks like, whether it's thriving or barely surviving. What I do know is it matters how we treat our spouse. As small as kindness may seem, it gives worth and sends a *big* message that you care. It's also a key that opens up the door to love—it has the ability to rekindle fading embers back to a hot and roaring fire! If you're struggling, admit your failure and tell your husband you're sorry. Ask God to help you change. I know without a doubt if He helped me, He'll help you too!

FAITH-FILLED IDEA: Date Night In

Put the children to bed a little earlier than usual. After they're all tucked in and asleep, serve a special meal to your man. Why not try our chicken Alfredo recipe on page 193 in the "HELPful Resources"? Be creative as you decorate—use a cute tablecloth and set the table with china, goblets, and a few candles to make it special and romantic. Try to be extra kind and enjoy some quality time together!

13

Don't Be a Scaredy Cat

·············· DEB WEAKLY ··············

*The LORD God said, "It is not good for the man to
be alone. I will make a helper suitable for him."*

Genesis 2:18

*Pity the married couple who expect
too much from one another.*

Ruth Bell Graham

I'm sad to say this, but before becoming a Christian, I made a lot of
mistakes, and I was terribly afraid my children would do the same.
This fear felt crippling, and it caused me to be hyperfocused on doing
everything just perfect so we could have a Christian home that popped
out little disciples for Jesus. During this discouraging season, I went to
every moms' conference I could, looking for the formula to help my
husband and me raise Christian kids.

In theory, this was a good idea, but while at these conferences, I
heard the speakers say things that made me upset at my husband's
"lack of spiritual leadership." They said if my husband wasn't reading
the Bible to our children every single day, going to a men's group at
church, or leading a certain way, he was falling short. And after all, if
he wasn't leading just the "right way," how could I follow him? Eager
to be the best Christian mom I could, I tried to implement every sug-
gestion they gave at the expense of my poor husband.

I came home from these conferences frustrated and disappointed
in him, telling him *all* the ways he was falling short. But truthfully, he

was leading; he simply led our family in his way, not in my way, or in the way of the "experts" I was listening to. As I began to look for what my husband was doing right, God showed me the many ways he was leading so well! He took us to church, he brought the kids with him to clean up the yard of an elderly neighbor or a single mom, and he prayed with us at night before the kids went to bed. Randy is a man of his word who honors his commitments, the pleasant and unpleasant ones, and he taught his kids to do the same. My husband was so faithful in leading our family, but for some reason, all I focused on was what he wasn't doing "right."

Thankfully, God spoke to my heart and showed me that Randy was doing a great job as the spiritual leader of our home, and I finally got out of his way and let him lead. Instead of complaining about what he wasn't doing, I started praying about becoming his helper. God answered this prayer by helping me find fun, simple devotions that Randy could read to our kids. I found easy ones that I could photocopy and cut into pieces of paper, and I put them in a jar with chocolate candy. After dinner, the kids and I loved to enjoy a piece of chocolate while Dad read the simple devotion out loud. Randy appreciated the help and soon felt more confident in discipling our children. I also began cooking a big breakfast on Sunday mornings, and while we ate, Randy would read a devotion or a chapter of the Bible in funny voices that made the Scriptures come alive to the kids. They loved it and have fond memories of Sunday morning devotions with their daddy!

When I stopped fussing at Randy and began to help him, he began to lead more confidently. As wives, we have the ability to help our men step into their calling to be a godly husband or cause them to feel defeated because of our nagging and complaining. We need to cheer them on and be their helpers, trusting that God will work in their hearts the way He wants to. What a blessing it is when we get out of the way and watch God work!

One last note: In this world, you will hear lots of voices trying to tell you exactly what you need to do in your home, but the beautiful voice we all need to tune into is the Holy Spirit. Ask Him to teach you and your husband what you need to know to raise your children up for Him. Even as you read this book, stop after each article and ask Jesus what He wants you to remember from each segment. We love the Help Club for Moms saying "You do you!" We all have different husbands, children, financial situations, personalities, and much more. God doesn't want us to all be the same. So ask Him for wisdom each day and listen for His answers. He is so faithful and will help you with any situation you need help with!

FAITH-FILLED IDEA: Resources for Devotions

If your family is looking for some great books to help make devotions easy, we have a list for you. Be sure to pray and ask God for tools to help you share Christ with your kids. He knows your family best and will give you exactly what you need! Please refer to page 188 in the "HELPful Resources."

14

The Greatest Gift You Can Give to Your Husband

TARA DAVIS

I pray that you, being rooted and established in love, may have power, together with all the Lord's holy people, to grasp how wide and long and high and deep is the love of Christ.

Ephesians 3:17-18

I can't promise you that marriage will be easy, but I can say that marriage, the way God intended it to be, is a treasure worth fighting for.

Darlene Schacht

There have been years of emptiness in my life. Years in which I desperately searched for the approval of others, just needing to know I was good enough. What a strange thing it is, looking to other broken people to fill the cracks in our own life. Who is whole enough to fill us in the way we need and good enough to love us in the way we desire? No human could help me figure out who I was and help me find peace with who I wasn't. And before I lifted my eyes to my Savior, I was alone, with a smile on my face while barely clinging to the shreds of my fractured heart.

Inside each of us is an empty vessel we long to have filled with worth. We seek to receive this value from many places. In search of our identity, we turn to relationships, accomplishments, or belief in ourselves. Often as wives, however, we hand this empty vessel to our husbands and ask them to fill it with our worth.

At this point, we become only as good as our husband's performance. When he has a bad day, we are shaken. When he struggles, our value plummets. When he fails to see us through the eyes of Christ, our identity is destroyed. But what if I told you this was never God's plan for you? If you have placed the vessel of your worth anywhere but securely with your loving Savior, you have placed it in the wrong hands.

When you find your identity anywhere but in the Lord, you are left empty, shallow, always searching for more of what you lack. When you attempt to gain your worth from your husband, you become selfish, always needing something from him, preoccupied with your longings and how he isn't fulfilling them adequately. You are not able to love like Jesus or walk in the glorious freedom His love offers!

When at last I was able to see myself through the eyes of my Savior, I could hear His truth about who I am as His child and I was able to allow Him to meet my needs according to His glorious riches (Philippians 4:19). Instead of allowing another imperfect human to determine my worth, I rested in the unconditional, unending love of my Creator, a love beyond anything imaginable (Ephesians 3:17-21). And His love makes me whole, filling in all the deep fissures in my heart with His tenderness and grace.

Sister, when you finally surrender your empty vessel to Christ and allow Him to fill you in a way only the God of the universe can, you gain the freedom to love your husband the way the Lord intended (1 John 4:19). Only then can you shine the light of Jesus to him in every circumstance and be the friend, lover, and helper the Lord has made you to be. You will be able to love your husband right where he is, struggles and all, and pray for him in a powerful way!

In fact, the very best gift you can give your husband is to pray that he will know the mighty, transforming love of the Lord. In Ephesians 3:14-19, Paul tells us that the ability to know the deep love of our Savior is only found through the power of the Holy Spirit. We must pray that our husbands will utilize the power of the Holy Spirit to know the vast height, depth, and width of God's love for them. We must pray that God will fill the emptiness within our husbands with His heart-healing love.

Sister, when you are able to walk the faithful path of total surrender to the Lord within your marriage, a deep, abiding joy awaits you (Colossians 3:12-15)! When you are no longer wrapped up in your worth and your needs but are fully occupied by the love of Christ and the act of pouring that love out to your husband, God can begin to heal and refine your marriage through His love! And that is a love that will change everything, my friend. Believe me.

FAITH-FILLED IDEA: Pray Ephesians 3:17-19

Write Ephesians 3:17-19 on a notecard and place it somewhere you will see it frequently. Pray this Scripture over your husband daily. Pray that your husband will know the love of Christ in his very core, that he will walk in Christ's love, and that he will live a life that is transformed by the love of Jesus. Pray also that you will intimately know this love and that you will find your worth in Him so you can begin to love your husband with the extravagant love of Christ.

15

Be a Student of Your Man

······· RAE-ELLEN SANDERS ·······

*Each man among you [without exception] is to love
his wife as his very own self [with behavior worthy
of respect and esteem, always seeking the best
for her with an attitude of loving kindness], and the
wife [must see to it] that she respects and delights
in her husband [that she notices him and prefers
him and treats him with loving concern, treasuring
him, honoring him, and holding him dear].*

Ephesians 5:33 AMP

To love your spouse is to invest in blue-chip stocks.

Gary Chapman

When my husband and I were newlyweds, we had our first argument the day after we got home from our honeymoon! As soon as we walked in the door, I plopped on the couch and kicked off my shoes to relax. Immediately, my husband looked at my shoes on the floor and asked me when I was going to put them away. "Why not put them away now?" Well, that's when our first spat began. I learned right from the beginning that my husband likes his home tidy, and though he does not demand this from me, we work better together when we understand each other's expectations and work as a team.

I have been married for nineteen years now, and my housecleaning skills have improved, but that didn't happen overnight—I had to work at it. Five children later, my husband realized that we couldn't keep our place picture perfect, so now I delegate some of the housework. However, I still do my best to intentionally please my husband in this area. Love is a sacrificial, unselfish choice in which you put another above yourself. It is an act of will that requires personal discipline. Let's face it—marriage takes work.

Be encouraged in this, friend: Christ loves your marriage and designed you to be your husband's helpmate. If you're like me, I need help being a "helpmate"! The good news is that God supports us by giving us guidelines in Scripture, examples through godly mentors, and wonderful Christian resources to read and study.

Recently, I read Gary Chapman's book, *The 5 Love Languages*. This book has helped me realize how I can love my husband better. Being knowledgeable of your spouse's love language and how to express love is vital in every marriage. My man's love language is "words of affirmation." Although what he says is nice and flattering, his words are not my love language. Don't get me wrong, I love the accolades, but love in action—known as "acts of service"—blesses me more. Now my husband will often run a bubble bath for me and tell the children that it's "mom time" so I can soak in peace. He has been known to buy my favorite chocolates and bring home flowers for no other reason than to show me his love in action.

Often, we try to fill our spouse's cup with what works best for filling our own. While I need acts of service to make me feel cherished, words of affirmation are equally important to express love to my husband. So I tell him daily how much I love him and appreciate his hard work and strong ethics. By acknowledging his positive traits, I fill my husband's cup and make him desire to be an even better provider, father, and lover.

What I've learned is that verbal appreciation can really change the climate of a marriage, but it's not enough! In fact, God's Word instructs us, "My children, our love should not be just words and talk; it must be true love, which shows itself in action" (1 John 3:18 GNT). My spouse and I have openly talked about what we can each do to make the other happy, and what we've discovered is that our needs are different. I am sure you and your spouse are wired differently too.

Interestingly, we have a primary love language and then secondary ones. Physical touch is also pretty important to my husband. I am sure this is top on the list for most men. You might just find your husband has more than one love language and that you do too! Continuing to love your spouse in his love language will give you confidence that you are enriching your marriage and just might spur your husband to please you in yours!

All of us feel loved in different ways. Does your spouse know your love language, and do you know his? If you haven't sat down to discuss this important topic, I encourage you to carve out intentional time to have this much needed conversation. Be a student of your man; take notes, and then make a strategic plan to execute a new way of showing love in action. Don't forget to take notice of what is effective! Challenge yourself to love your husband with his love language and watch your marriage soar.

FAITH-FILLED IDEA: A Special Dinner

I mentioned my honeymoon earlier; it brings back such fond recollections of good Italian food, especially a shared favorite called bruschetta! Ripe tomatoes served over crusty bread with large basil leaves eaten among the cobblestones of Venice and Rome. Ah, the memories! We still order this when we go out on special occasions, but this is easy enough to re-create at home. Try Brandi's recipe on page 194.

16

Intimacy in Marriage

KRYSTLE PORTER

Do nothing out of selfish ambition or vain conceit. Rather, in humility value others above yourselves, not looking to your own interests but each of you to the interests of others.

Philippians 2:3-4

To love another person is to see the face of God.

**From the musical *Les Miserables*,
English translation by Herbert Kretzmer**

In the early years of my marriage, I can distinctly recall being afraid of real intimacy. Not the intimacy portrayed in movies, but the intimacy that comes from knowing someone body and soul. I had some heartbreaking times as a young girl where people took advantage of this precious part of me. Because of that, it was easy to disconnect and, honestly, just neglect this area of my marriage. Over the years, I have had to dive into the Bible to learn about what true intimacy looks like within the context of marriage and trust that God's plan for the closeness that comes through intimacy in my marriage was good!

Gently and lovingly, God changed my heart. As I became a little more vulnerable year after year, God showed me that I was capable of giving to my husband in this way, and He blessed my marriage when I did. My husband and I are coming up on fourteen years of marriage, and the level of intimacy that I once was afraid of and thought to be out of reach is a living reality. We don't always get it right, but it does happen more often than not!

If your story resembles mine in any way or you are struggling to be intimate with your husband, be gentle to yourself. Lasting change and growth is done slowly, over time. It is not driven by guilt, and it cannot be rushed. Jesus is going to meet you right where you are. Sometimes He helps us by nudging us to see that counselor, to talk to that friend, or to simply embrace the words written for us in the Bible.

Intimacy does not usually occur casually. It is something that is fostered and cared for, with intentionality and love. It is not something that automatically happens when we marry our spouses. It is built up over time. As it grows, it becomes deeply rooted in the foundation of our relationship. God has made this act of love something that is to be cherished and enjoyed. There is power in coming together.

I have had the most success when I have implemented the following simple yet powerful rhythms to my marriage to keep the fire burning (or start the fire!). I have also found that the more I practice intimacy and am intentional, the easier it becomes and the more connected I feel to my sweet husband.

Schedule times to be intimate. It may not seem like the most romantic thing ever suggested, but friend, it works! I remember as a young twentysomething being in a small group at church and an older couple sharing that this concept worked for them in their marriage. I thought they were crazy! But you know what? Their love permeated from them when they were in the room. Keep in mind, every marriage has its own rhythm; your intimate life doesn't need to look like anyone else's! Do what makes sense for you and seems realistic for your relationship with your man. Set a few reminders and dates on your phone or calendar and follow through!

Think about your man during the day. Thinking of your man throughout the day and remembering why you once said your vows and how much your husband loves you and your family is a powerful way to kindle the fire! Thinking of sex can prepare your mind and heart and create a healthy longing for your spouse. What was missing might be replaced with anticipation. I have noticed that when a couple is out of the practice of coming together (because of busyness or disinterest), intentional planning makes all the difference and brings them closer every single time.

Be an initiator! Don't wait for your husband to ask for intimacy. Some men will give up on asking. Show him you love him by being interested in him first. It will speak volumes to your husband when you make the first move. As ladies, we often want our men to pursue us. And this is not a bad thing! But sometimes, it's tricky. If we leave all the initiating to our men, we may miss out on some sweet time of unity and connection. God is so good, and He may very well use your efforts in this area to be the change that your intimacy needs!

Pray for the Lord's guidance. We know intimacy can be complicated. Maybe your relationship, as it stands today, isn't where you would like it to be. Or maybe you have deep hurts that need to be resolved. I want to say to you that there is always hope with Jesus in whatever season we find ourselves in. God is our Healer. He can work a precious miracle in your life to mend past wounds and to rebuild your marriage. Don't be afraid to partner with Him; prayer is powerful!

FAITH-FILLED IDEA: Initiate Intimacy

Initiate intimacy with your husband this week! Pray and ask God how He can help you make this a sweet time of love and connection for the two of you. Why not start in the kitchen with a man-pleasing recipe—"Southwest Egg Rolls" found on page 196—followed by additional rolling around in the bedroom!

17

Loving Your Husband Even When He Is Unlovable

RACHEL JONES

Be completely humble and gentle; be patient, bearing with one another in love.

Ephesians 4:2

A mentor told me early on, "Beth, if you treat that man like he already is everything you want him to become, he'll become it." I could have cut my husband down with my tongue, but I didn't think that was wise. A man needs his woman's love and respect.

Beth Moore

Showing love to our husbands when we are disappointed in them or they have hurt us is hard. It seems completely impossible. Unlovable behavior deserves harshness and sharp words...at least, that is what the world tells us. My friend, every marriage goes through times when it seems impossible to find the joy you had in those early years. Seasons of struggle are normal, but we need not become discouraged. It is during these times in our marriage when we need to respond not only in obedience to God but in a noticeably different way than the world does. We need to respond in peace because a righteous and loving tone is a precursor to the hope our marriages so desperately need.

There have been many, many times in my marriage when my

husband has been unlovable; he is human after all. I have had ample opportunities to overlook annoyances, but guess what? I struggle with keeping my mouth shut. Learning to love my husband has taught me the most about myself. Looking back, it was often my heart that needed tending to. My wicked, self-centered heart, which made hurtful comments and showed no empathy. This powerful verse has convicted me and helped me focus on the state of my own heart: "For out of the abundance of the heart his mouth speaks" (Luke 6:45 ESV). For years, I would not even consider what was going on in my husband's heart for him to act in such frustrating or unlovable ways; I only focused on myself. How annoyed I felt, how inconvenienced I was, how I needed him and he wasn't there for me. I realized I had lost a lot of compassion and general goodwill toward my husband. Even though I was let down, it was *me*, in turn, who was letting him down.

Our marriage began to vastly improve when I started living out these verses in Colossians 3:13-14 (ESV): "Bearing with one another and, if one has a complaint against another, forgiving each other; as the Lord has forgiven you, so you also must forgive. And above all these put on love, which binds everything together in perfect harmony." Simply put, I needed to become more tender and compassionate toward my husband; and I needed to lean into the Holy Spirit for the strength to do it. Here are three things I have learned about showing unconditional love to my husband:

My husband is a good man! And at some level, yours is too. Even if he is not half the man you want him to be, you should still treat him like he is a good man. Look at the quote from Beth Moore today. Treating your husband like the man you desire him to be will cause him to work hard to live up to your expectations! Your husband longs to make you happy (even if he rarely shows it), and you need to be his biggest cheerleader. He is your husband and deserves your love and support.

I am often unlovable too! Can we all just make a commitment to accept our humanness and not act like our husbands are the only annoying ones? Apologize to your hubby often, and he will likely do the same. Be the first person to start a conversation toward forgiveness. Be more selfless and realize that a happy and healthy marriage can start with *you*. Stop the blame game and pray about the possibility that the Lord is trying to teach you something about yourself. I know when I admitted my unlovable qualities to my husband out loud (it was so hard!), he really appreciated it and wanted to respond by doing the same.

I can do nothing apart from the Holy Spirit. Period. There is little else to say on this matter except stop trying to improve your husband! Just stop! It is not your job. Your husband belongs to the Lord. You have been given the amazing blessing to respect him, honor him, and love him for your whole life. It is an incredible gift from God to be married, and we need to find hope in the trust we have in Him. Proverbs 3:5-6 says, "Trust in the LORD with all your heart and lean not on your own understanding; in all your ways submit to him, and he will make your paths straight."

FAITH-FILLED IDEA: List What You Love

Journal for a few minutes about what you love most about your husband. Think of his best qualities and his strengths, and list them all out. This is important because it reminds us why we fell in love with and married our husbands years ago. Turn to it in times of confusion, and it can be a sort of anchor to your marriage.

18

Respect: One of Your Man's Most Important Needs

························· DEB WEAKLY ·························

However, each one of you also must love his wife as he loves himself, and the wife must respect her husband.

Ephesians 5:33

There is no more lovely, friendly and charming relationship, communion or company than a good marriage.

Martin Luther

Not too long ago, my husband and I went on a date to a local restaurant. I was looking over the menu when I noticed a couple in their sixties about to sit in the booth next to us. They sat down next to each other on the same side of the booth. The woman looked cute and classy, but the one thing I noticed about her (after I saw that she was married) was the way she turned her body so she could really look into her husband's eyes and listen intently to every word he said. This went on the whole time they were together. It impressed me so much to see how she was paying complete attention to him and put her hand on his every now and then. I loved that! Here they were, an older couple, still in love, and she was still showing him respect by truly listening to him and looking into his eyes.

After being married for twenty-eight years, I have become more and more aware of how much my husband really needs me to respect him. God teaches us about respect in Ephesians 5:33: "Each one of you must love his wife as he loves himself, and the wife must respect her husband." The Amplified Bible says, "The wife [must see to it] that she respects and delights in her husband [that she notices him and prefers him and treats him with loving concern, treasuring him, honoring him, and holding him dear]."

Isn't that beautiful? God wants you to respect and delight in your husband: to notice him, prefer him, treat him with loving concern, treasure him, honor him, and hold him dear. Wow, how romantic! I know this verse may be challenging, especially if you do not feel truly loved by your husband. Pray for him. Pray for your marriage, for the love to return, and then do your best to respect your man. Ask God to help you talk sweetly to him and to encourage him.

Our husbands also need us to be their cheerleaders; they need to feel that we think they are the smartest men on the face of the earth. In our home, we call it "feeling their muscles." It means that we praise the guys in our home (our sons need respect too). There is always something good to praise someone for. If you truly can't think of anything good to say about your husband, ask God to help you see his heart and to praise him. So often, people will rise to our expectations.

Does your man go to work every day? Does he come home every night? Does he spend time with the kids? When my children were growing up, I used to thank my husband for taking our family to church. I know there are a lot of men who would rather watch football or sleep in, but my man takes us to church.

Another thing I have noticed is that our men need us to affirm them in front of other people. Don't bash your man in front of others or behind his back. It's no fun to be put down or made fun of. "Do unto others as you would have them do unto you." Ask God to help you be the wise woman that builds her house and not the foolish woman who tears it down with her own hands (Proverbs 14:1).

Sister, accept your husband and your own puzzle. Our men need us to appreciate them and to bring life to our homes. That's what we do as women—we bring life. Ask God to help you love your husband, respect him, and be more content with who he is and your life together.

FAITH-FILLED IDEA: Meet Him at the Door

One of my favorite habits when our kids were growing up was going to the door to meet my husband when he arrived home from work. I remember learning this tip from an older, wiser woman named Emilie Barnes, who said, "Your husband could have gone anywhere else after work, but he chose to come home to you. Make his homecoming special. If you're in the middle of a diaper change, wrap that diaper around that baby's bottom and go welcome your man." Our children remember their dad's homecoming with fondness—going to the door and clapping and cheering "Daddy, Daddy, Daddy!" when he walked inside. I believe it's one of the reasons they truly respect their dad. When we honor and respect our husbands, chances are that our kids will too.

19

Praying Through Tough Times

*I urge, then, first of all, that petitions, prayers,
intercession and thanksgiving be made for all people.*

1 Timothy 2:1

*We are never more like Christ than
in prayers of intercession.*

Austin Phelps

Several years ago, I came to a place of desperation in my marriage. My husband was facing some hard situations and, as much as I hated to see him struggle, there was not one thing I could do to change his circumstances. I was at a loss and had nowhere to turn but to God. My husband needed my prayers, but I just didn't know how to pray effectively. I wanted to do more than bring a list of needs before the Lord; I wanted to see the mountains move.

Then I remembered one of my sisters recommending that I read *The Circle Maker* by Mark Batterson.[3] Out of a deep desire to change, I checked out the book and the audiobook from the library; I needed answers, and I was determined to find them! Before I read, I prayed and committed to myself, "This will not be a book on prayer I read and then forget. This book will change my life."

I listened to *The Circle Maker* several times on audiobook and let the message go deep into my soul. As much as I wanted a formula for the right way to pray, I learned that there is no special prayer to move

God's heart. Praying to move the mountains is about believing we serve a big God who is all powerful and can make *all* things right. He shows us His omnipotent power repeatedly throughout the Scriptures. He has the power to heal, the power to restore, and the power to bless. Our job as daughters of the Most High God is to trust Him to hear our prayers and to continue to pray in faith for what we are contending for. He says, "Ask and it will be given to you; seek and you will find; knock and the door will be opened to you" (Matthew 7:7). We serve a Good Father who will not give us a stone when we ask for bread (Matthew 7:9-11). His Word says He will give good things to those who ask! Moms, we must believe not only that He is able but that He loves us and wants to answer our prayers.

During this time, I discovered that there is power in praying God's promises found in the Bible. As I spent time in the Word, I realized how much I loved praying the Scriptures I was reading over my husband. One of my favorite Scriptures to pray became Psalm 5:12: "Surely, LORD, you bless the righteous; you surround them with your favor as with a shield." I love thinking about God's blessing and favor surrounding my husband as I pray. Along with praying the Scriptures, I would bring my husband's needs before the Lord, thus "circling" him in prayer.

Whether your husband needs healing, wisdom, revelation, or a miracle, you can "circle" him in prayer by praying the promises of God and bringing his needs before the Lord. But remember, praying for your husband through the tough times is not about finding the right words to say—it is about believing that God loves your husband more than you do and that He has good things in store for both of you!

It has been more than five years since I began this journey of intentionally praying for my husband, casting all my cares on Him because He cares for me (1 Peter 5:7). I have seen God answer my prayers in small ways, in big ways, and in ways I never imagined possible, and He will do the same for you. Be bold, believe, and ask God to do big things!

FAITH-FILLED IDEA: Find Help to Pray

While there is no formula, the Bible says, "The Spirit helps us in our weakness. We do not know what we ought to pray for, but the Spirit himself intercedes for us" (Romans 8:26). Not only can we pray Scripture over our husbands and families (the book of Psalms is a great place to start), but there are also Christian resources that can lead us and guide us in our prayers. One of my favorites is Stormie Omartian's book *The Power of a Praying Wife*.[4] It is broken into thirty topical chapters so you can pray one topic each day of the month. You can pray the prayer she has written or create your own, adding your husband's specific needs as the Holy Spirit leads you.

20

Lavish Grace on Your Man

KRYSTLE PORTER

*God has given each of you a gift from his great variety
of spiritual gifts. Use them well to serve one another.*

1 Peter 4:10 NLT

*Let the wife make the husband glad to come home,
and let him make her sorry to see him leave.*

Martin Luther

When my husband and I were newly married, I remember one evening, very vividly, where we were sitting at the dinner table arguing. I cannot for the life of me remember what the quarrel was about, but I recall being so angry with him that I nudged my plate about six inches away from me and said, "Forget you!" It didn't seem to do the trick or incite the kind of response in him I was hoping for (he is very calm by nature). Then I stormed out of the front door of our little condo, sat down on a step about twenty feet away, and pouted for a bit.

I thought that he would for sure come out, plead his apologies, and beg for me to come back inside. He never did. I waited there for what felt like hours, though it was likely thirty minutes or so. I remember sitting there thinking, "Is this how marriage is supposed to feel? I thought it was supposed to make you feel good." I remember feeling very defeated. I knew in that moment my perspective needed to change.

Marriage is about two sinful people learning to live together in companionship. We don't always get it right. We can try our very best, but perfection is reserved for Jesus only. Thank goodness for that! So many expectations can be released when you allow your spouse to just be another person in this world—trying his best but inevitably falling short. There is an immeasurable opportunity to love our spouses well by living a life that overflows with grace for this very reason.

I looked up the definition of the word "grace," and one source said, "The condition or fact of being favored by someone." What a beautiful concept! Which leads me to my next definition; what is favor? It is an act of kindness beyond what is due or usual. Grace should be poured upon our spouses in bucketfuls. If you have an issue with your man that you want Him to repent of, your kindness toward him, your undeserved "favor," may be just what God is calling you to do to help him out of his pit!

Here are two wonderful ways we can extend grace to our husbands:

Learn to accept your husband's limitations. "For all have sinned and fall short of the glory of God" (Romans 3:23). Friend, this is a huge one. Like I mentioned above, our husbands will not, and cannot, be perfect, and neither can you or I. Our men have their own set of strengths and weaknesses that make them who they are. Over time, I have grown to laugh and even enjoy my husband's imperfections. Their vulnerability is a window into their heart. Don't take that for granted! Pray for him and love him through his struggles, even if these struggles affect your relationship. Before you try to "fix" anything about your husband, go to God in devoted prayer—not just a frustrated, disgruntled prayer, but pour out your heart before the Lord. You can rest easy that Jesus can do more than you expect or hope in the situation.

Always assume the best. "A fool takes no pleasure in understanding, but only in expressing his opinion" (Proverbs 18:2 ESV). When you decide to assume the best in your spouse, the whole tone of your relationship will change. It creates trust when you feel like you are on the same team instead of on opposing ones. Conversations become a lot more graceful, and protective walls come down. Assume your husband loves you and cares for you, even when he is bringing up something that's not fun to talk about and maybe even in a way that doesn't feel very loving. Decide ahead of time that you will actively listen instead of pleading your individual case in the argument. Bend your ear to understanding instead of winning. When you decide to trust and not assume the worst in your spouse, conversations that could possibly have turned into arguments become opportunities to grow closer. They may not deserve this, but showing them how much you love them by assuming the best will speak volumes.

FAITH-FILLED IDEA: Win as a Team

Around our house, we know that when one of us wins an argument, we both lose. So we focus on making sure that Team Porter (our last name) wins every disagreement. Together we come to a solution that allows us to both "win" and draws us closer because of it. Conflict is normal in a marriage, and we are presented with opportunities to either show love through forgiveness or stay defensive. So what team are you on? Pray about being on "Team _____" with your man. When a disagreement arises, quietly pray "God help me to be on Team _____, and to not only plead my case." This simple prayer could be a game changer for you! After all, Jesus is in the business of changing hearts.

21

Encouragement for Single Moms

The Spirit of the Sovereign Lord is on me, because the Lord has anointed me to proclaim good news to the poor. He has sent me to bind up the brokenhearted, to proclaim freedom for the captives and release from darkness for the prisoners, to proclaim the year of the Lord's favor and the day of vengeance of our God, to comfort all who mourn, and provide for those who grieve in Zion—to bestow on them a crown of beauty instead of ashes, the oil of joy instead of mourning, and a garment of praise instead of a spirit of despair. They will be called Oaks of Righteousness, a planting of the Lord for the display of his splendor.

Isaiah 61:1-3

This unmistakable peace of Jesus serves as a nourishing and healing balm against this hurting world, allowing us to endure and even thrive under hardship. It enables us to weep with hope, suffer with love, and die with joy.

Michelle Lynn Senters, *The Unseen Companion: God with the Single Mother*

We know the road you are walking as a single mom is not easy. The pressures of being a single mom may seem overwhelming at times. Perhaps you feel as if you are drowning, just one breath away from collapse. But sister, Jesus wants to rescue you! He loves you, treasures you and wants to lead you on this path of single motherhood. He wants you to know how precious you are to Him and that He walks closely alongside you every step of the way, gently unfolding the purpose of your life.

Let Him lead you in those purposes, my friend. Seek Him daily through His Word and through prayer. Let the whispers of the Holy Spirit ring louder in your ears than the deafening shouts of this world. He loves you so much that He even has your name engraved on the palm of His hand (Isaiah 49:16)! You are His, let that sink into your soul and become forever enough.

Even still, you may feel as if life has not turned out as you had planned. Perhaps, as in Isaiah 61:1-3, you are the one who is brokenhearted, the one who mourns. You may look at your life and see only ashes. But there is good news in this passage—Christ has come to bind your broken heart, to bring freedom in your life, to comfort you, provide for you, and give you a crown of beauty and joy! *You* are the oak of righteousness created for His splendor (Isaiah 61:3). Girl, *now it is time for you to grow!*

Let this truth take root in your heart today: God wants you, my friend, and every bit of you. There is nothing about you that He can't handle, nothing that causes Him to turn His loving eye away from you. He sees every bit of you through the sacrifice of Jesus and will never leave you nor forsake you (Deuteronomy 31:6). As a Christ-follower, you are *His girl*…forever.

You are completely and unconditionally His, but it doesn't end there. You have this one life to live for Jesus, to shine the light of His glory! All other aspirations or desires fade into the background as you look into His face, as you see His goodness and love for you. When you deny your old prideful, selfish nature and give every bit of yourself to Him, He can do huge things in you and through you. Living completely for Jesus is the most exciting journey upon which you will ever embark, and that adventure can begin for you today.

Yet if the path you are walking still seems dark and lonely, we want you to know you are never alone. Above all, you have your compassionate Savior carrying you through each moment of your day, but you also have Christian sisters standing alongside you, praying for you, and cheering you on! We want to bless you with a shoulder to lean on and some extra special encouragement, so we have created an inspiring weeklong journey that will help bring you closer than ever before to the heart of your Savior.

....

FAITH-FILLED IDEA: Take a Seven-Day Journey

....

For encouragement in your journey, turn to page 188 in the "HELPful Resources" for the "Seven-Day Journey to a Closer Walk with Jesus for the Single Mom."

Scriptures to Pray for Your Husband

Pray that your husband will know the depth of God's love for him.

> "[That you] may have power, together with all the Lord's holy people, to grasp how wide and long and high and deep is the love of Christ" (Ephesians 3:18).

Pray that your husband lives in accordance with God's calling for his life.

> "As a prisoner for the Lord, then, I urge you to live a life worthy of the calling you have received. Be completely humble and gentle; be patient, bearing with one another in love" (Ephesians 4:1-2).

Pray that the Lord will bless your husband's work.

> "Do you see someone skilled in their work? They will serve before kings; they will not serve before officials of low rank" (Proverbs 22:29).

Pray that God will make your husband a man of integrity.

> "The integrity of the upright guides them, but the unfaithful are destroyed by their duplicity" (Proverbs 11:3).

Pray that he will be filled with compassion, kindness, humility, gentleness, and patience.

> "Therefore, as God's chosen people, holy and dearly loved, clothe yourselves with compassion, kindness, humility, gentleness and patience" (Colossians 3:12).

Pray that your husband will desire wisdom and seek it diligently.

> "If any of you lacks wisdom, you should ask God, who gives generously to all without finding fault, and it will be given to you" (James 1:5).

Pray that your husband will trust in the Lord for his strength.

> "The LORD is my strength and my shield; my heart trusts in him, and he helps me" (Psalm 28:7).

Pray that he will stand up for what is right and defend the weak.

> "Learn to do right; seek justice. Defend the oppressed. Take up the cause of the fatherless; plead the case of the widow" (Isaiah 1:17).

Pray that God will strengthen your husband to resist temptation.

> "No temptation has overtaken you except what is common to mankind. And God is faithful; he will not let you be tempted beyond what you can bear. But when you are tempted, he will also provide a way out so that you can endure it" (1 Corinthians 10:13).

Pray that your husband will love God with his whole heart.

> "Love the LORD your God with all your heart and with all your soul and with all your strength" (Deuteronomy 6:5).

Part 3

The Wise Woman Loves Her Children

Sweet sister, raising your children for God is holy work.

As Christian moms, our greatest work is raising up children who know and love Jesus. What you do every day—discipling your children, wiping noses, breaking up sibling squabbles, cleaning up after yet another meal, or lying in bed at night with your child while they tell you their latest pondering—all this is kingdom work. You are raising up the next generation of Christians who will then raise up the next generation of Christians.

No matter how many times the world around us says that being a mom doesn't matter, we know the truth: Our work affects eternity. By staying faithful and loving your family well in the power of the Holy Spirit, you are sending a message of love forward to a time you will not see. Your grandchildren and great-grandchildren will thank you for the hard work you are doing today. They will have better lives because of the love you shared and the Christian life you passed on to your kids. When there is a mom in the home who has faith in the power of God in her children's lives, there's no stopping what she can do with her kids!

Mama, your love for your family pleases the Lord. Someday, you will know the impact of all your work. But for now, keep going, keep trying, keep believing, and keep praying, and by your faith, you will hear, "Well done, good and faithful servant."

love, Deb

22

Becoming a Wise Mom

· DEB WEAKLY ·

The wise woman builds her house.

Proverbs 14:1

*Wisdom is doing now what you are
going to be happy with later on.*

Joyce Meyer

abor and delivery do not come easy for me. I tried delivering our children naturally, but in both cases, the babies went into distress and I had to have Cesarean sections. I felt so discouraged when the moment came to wheel me into the operating room. With my first baby, I didn't even get to see her until an hour and a half after she was born, so she was sound asleep when they finally brought her to me. I delighted in holding my precious Christie, but it was super hard to nurse because I couldn't wake her up.

However, God gave me a gift with my second born. I remember laying in the recovery room and asking the nurse if there was any way they could bring my baby in so I could see him. The nurse wasn't supportive, and in a grouchy, matter-of-fact tone that I still remember today, she said, "I've been working in this hospital for twenty years and have never seen a baby come in the C-Section recovery room." I started to cry. Five minutes later, the tears stopped as I saw a different nurse walk through the electric doors carrying my baby. I remember feeling overwhelmed with joy as she placed Jack into my arms. All I could do was admire my wide-awake baby, who latched on and nursed right away. I will never forget that moment. It truly was a miracle.

As I look back on those experiences, I realize that my deliveries were just the beginning of the ups and downs of life with kids. Many experiences, such as childbirth, are out of our control, but others, such as the day-in-and-day-out routines of life lived with kids, can be cultivated intentionally with wisdom and help from Jesus. Your life will never be perfect, but for the most part, your life can be really beautiful, especially when you walk with the Lord one day at a time.

At the Help Club for Moms, we love and center our ministry on Proverbs 14:1: "The wise woman builds her house." It's a powerful Scripture which exhorts us to become wise women who look after their family and homes in a beautiful, life-giving way. I remember reading this verse as a young mom and desperately desiring to be wise and have a happy Christian family. I wanted a peaceful home centered on Christ where my family would love to reside, but I didn't know where to begin. As I began to search the Scriptures, I found the transformational verse James 1:5, "If any of you lacks wisdom, you should ask God, who gives generously to all without finding fault, and it will be given to you." Our God is generous and wants to help us become wise moms, and all we have to do is ask! When I finally understood this simple truth, I started praying first thing in the morning, asking God for wisdom and help.

I can now look back on my life and see the blessings of regularly asking God for wisdom and seeing the answers He provided. My life has definitely not been perfect; we have had our fair share of struggles, but perfection is not the goal anyway. Living each day staying close to Jesus by talking to Him and asking for His help is a beautiful way to live your life. And when you make a mistake, He is right there to pick you back up and help you move forward on the path He has for you. There will always be bumps in this life, but with God's wisdom and your obedience, you will definitely have more peace.

Sweet sister, take a moment right now and ask God to help you become the wise woman who builds her house. Tell Him you want His help to look back on your life and be pleased with the way you lived each day. If you've made mistakes (like we all have), simply pray and ask God for forgiveness and the help to make good choices in the power of the Holy Spirit. Remember, there is no condemnation for those who are in Christ Jesus (Romans 8:1). As a Christ-follower, you are forgiven and free, ready to take on each new day with the help of God. You can do it, mama!

FAITH-FILLED IDEA: Pray the Powerful Three

My husband's great-uncle, John Bass, is a wonderful man of God who was the former CEO of the Christian Booksellers Association. He was my spiritual dad and taught me much of what I know about leadership. Once, I asked him what has been the biggest contributor to his amazing life in the Lord. He said, "For the last thirty years, I have prayed and asked God for three things daily: wisdom, knowledge, and compassion."

I started praying and asking God for these three things about fifteen years ago, and it has made a huge difference in my life. There have been many situations in my life where the wisdom I possessed could only have come from God. He has been so faithful to answer this prayer, and my life is a testimony to His generosity in how He has answered. Try praying for the powerful three in your life, and watch God work these traits in your life too.

23

Daily Discipleship for Children

TARA DAVIS

*These commandments that I give you today
are to be on your hearts. Impress them on
your children. Talk about them when you sit
at home and when you walk along the road,
when you lie down and when you get up.*

Deuteronomy 6:6-7

*The cost of discipleship is high, but the cost
of non-discipleship is even higher.*

David Platt

Upon embarking on this journey of motherhood, I honestly felt so overwhelmed. Often, the magnitude of being mama to these little ones and teaching them about Jesus seemed staggering. Some days, I wished I could find a "better" mom to raise my kids—you know, a mom who really knew what she was doing and had her act together. Oh, how I have prayed and begged the Lord to help me raise these three boys of mine in a way that shines with the grace of Jesus. Guess what? I still don't know what I'm doing, but God is showing me how to hold His hand as He directs me in motherhood and prompts me to glean wisdom from His Word and the direction of the Holy Spirit (Isaiah 40:11).

Maybe you are like me; maybe you are confused and searching desperately for guidance on how to raise your own little (or big) ones. There are so many voices in today's culture beckoning us as mothers, each promising easy answers and quick fixes. If we are not careful, we will find ourselves drowning in guilt, chasing perfection in one parenting formula after another. But listen closely friend, do you hear that? There is a still, small voice, filled with freedom and ringing clear above the rest. It is the voice of the Lord, calling you as a mom to learn from Him alone and to find peace in the goodness of His ways.

Mama, He will help you raise your little ones in a way that draws them to the heart of Jesus. He will show you how to daily disciple your children, teaching them to become worshippers of God and encouraging them to become satisfied in His love. And He will help them grow into individuals who are awestruck by the King of the universe and who find their worth in Him alone! And here is the key: All you need to do is just follow Him, one step at a time, day after day, as you raise these little ones whom He has entrusted to you.

He will give you unique wisdom for your own individual children, but there is one thing we can count on, God wants us to teach each and every one of our kids about Him. He tells us in Deuteronomy 6 to involve Him in every aspect of our children's day and to train them in His ways. As parents, we are the only people in the lives of our little ones charged with directing them on the path of righteousness. Sister, we must feed our children on the living Word of God (Jeremiah 15:16)!

But how do we even approach a task so huge? The same way we approach the remainder of parenting: one small step at a time. A little of God's Word and a dose of worship, shared with our kids day after day leads to a childhood rich in the truths of the Lord! Choose a time each day during which you can delve into the Scripture with your kids. Make it a habit to read a children's devotional during breakfast, sing a hymn before lunch, or discuss a Proverb during snack. Little habits like this will encourage a lifelong pursuit of Jesus for your kids.

Finally, do not forget that in order to disciple your children in the Word and ways of Jesus, you must spend time with Him daily as well! Like a water pitcher, you cannot pour out unless you are filled yourself. Read God's Word and share what you are learning with your children. Have a little basket close by with things your kids can do during your quiet time—a comic book Bible such as *The Action Bible* or *The Picture*

Bible, a journal in which they can write or draw, or coloring pages that tell the stories of God's Word are all options to encourage your children to join you during your quiet time. When they see you enjoying God's Word, it will appeal to them all the more.

God is equipping you to bring Christ into your family life. His yoke is easy and His burden is light (Matthew 11:28-30). One day at a time, He will give you the wisdom and desire you need to direct your children into His arms. Keep going, mama! This task may seem large, even overwhelming at times, but you have a loving Father who will take you by the hand and lead you every step of the way.

FAITH-FILLED IDEA: Full Tummies, Full Hearts

Can I let you in on my secret to discipleship with my kids? Food. My kids are a captive audience any time they are eating! During meal time, they happily soak up the Bible, beautiful devotions, Scripture memory, and praise songs. I keep a basket of books by our table so I have everything I need at my fingertips (find some great ideas for what to do during this time on page 188). Why don't you give it a try? Pop something delicious into the oven, such as the quiche found on page 206, and let your kids fill their tummies while you fill their hearts with the Word of God.

24

Prayers for a Busy Mom

KRYSTLE PORTER

*For everything there is a season, and a
time for every matter under heaven.*

Ecclesiastes 3:1 ESV

*I pray because the need flows out of
me all the time, waking and sleeping. It
doesn't change God, it changes me.*

C.S. Lewis

t was 6:00 a.m. on a warm, Arizona summer day. The sun was still hiding behind the mountains, but surprisingly, I was awake before the kids. I tiptoed my way through the house toward the kitchen, put the kettle on to heat water for some hot tea, and lit a candle on the coffee table. The house was calm and peaceful. I opened up my Bible and started to read from Proverbs. I immediately felt my body release stress as I sank into the couch and began to ponder God's Word.

Then it happened; my three-year-old was rubbing her eyes sleepily, hair disheveled, and was walking down the hall toward me. My first reaction was to be angry; I hadn't even had my tea yet! But my second reaction was to snuggle that little cutie and have a few moments of alone time with her before the rest of the house woke up. But one thing was for sure, my moment of peace had passed and my "mom hat" was put on for the day.

It seems that even when we are intentional to set aside time to pray and just be in the presence of Jesus, there are always children needing us. I remember the time before kids when I could sit down to pray and journal to my heart's content with no distractions! I miss those days. But in this new season with little ones, uninterrupted time is often unrealistic even with the best attempts. All the while, I know that my need for time with Jesus is more important than ever with these precious ones to take care of! So what is a mom to do?

As busy moms, sometimes it's hard to figure out when we have time to pray. Over the years, I have found that there is almost no perfect time to pray. There will always be interruptions with children around. While this can be frustrating at times, it also urges us to get creative! We have to find a way to have those "little distractions" actually work for us and not against us. (See the faith-filled idea on the next page!)

Not too long ago, I was having a particularly chaotic day, which led me to be being grumpy and irritable. I was rushing around the house, cleaning up what felt like a billion toys. I had a list of things that needed to get done and dinner that had to be made. I hadn't showered for the day, and I just felt completely overwhelmed. As I was barking orders at my kids, I (loudly) said to my oldest (who was seven years old), "Mommy is in a *bad* mood today, and I just need you guys to clean and listen!"

My daughter came over to me very sweetly and said, "Mom, is it okay if I pray for you? I think God could help your heart feel better." Then she prayed a short little prayer for me and, wow, did it help! My seven-year-old's prayer truly encouraged my heart. There were so many times she and I would pray together when she was having a rough day, in spite of all my busyness, and she got it. She saw the value and blessing of prayer, and her seven-year-old little heart wanted to extend that to me too!

Sweet mom, our short but heartfelt prayers for and with our children matter so much to God. He hears each and every one and cares deeply. He sees us. He knows our season and loves us all the more for it. Busy prayers lifted to an almighty God are never in vain. We also never know what kind of impact our little prayers are making in the hearts of our sweet kids. I suspect it's more than we realize. Who knew that on a day that I needed help, my own prayers would soon be answered by my seven-year-old, who was paying close attention to her mama!

"Let us not become weary in doing good, for at the proper time we will reap a harvest if we do not give up" (Galatians 6:9).

Our prayers with our children hold just as much weight to the Lord as our prayers said in solitude. So if you are having a day where you aren't able to have that alone time with Jesus, do not fret! God is so good. He totally gets our busy seasons with little ones (or big ones) and loves each and every prayer we offer up to Him! You may look back and those prayers said amid tiny toddler hands, or that teenager with a wounded heart, may be your very favorite ones.

We should learn to embrace this unique season of prayer with kids in tow!

FAITH-FILLED IDEA: Pray These Prayers

We have a great list that you can fervently pray for and with your children despite your busyness. Go to page 201 in the "HELPful Resources" for five simple and fun ways to pray!

25

Reaching Your Child's Heart

RACHEL JONES

A gentle answer turns away wrath, but a harsh word stirs up anger. The tongue of the wise adorns knowledge, but the mouth of the fool gushes folly.

Proverbs 15:1-2

To handle yourself, use your head; to handle others, use your heart.

Eleanor Roosevelt

R aising children is a complete joy. It is a journey filled with laughter, happiness, frustration, and in my case, some severe regret. During my early years of motherhood, there were some moments that I wish I could go back and change. You see, friends, I struggle with my anger. Well, let me clarify; I really used to struggle with my anger toward my children. However, the Lord has done a huge work in my heart, and anger is something I have battled against fiercely.

When my girls were toddlers and started becoming more like real people, my life became more difficult. It felt more difficult because they started really getting into things and making mistakes, and I started losing my patience all too often. I remember in those days that little things like a spill in the kitchen would often cause me to lose my temper, especially on a busy day. Looking back, it took only five minutes to clean up the mess, but it took much longer to mend my daughter's broken spirit after I had scolded her. If I wasn't careful, I would slowly start causing a wedge to build up between my daughters and myself.

Over the years, I have had to submit my temper and anger to the Lord. And He has been so good! He revealed to me what an honor it is to be a mom and has helped me to remain calm and lean on Him when I am tempted to become angry at my girls for something minor. Most importantly, He spoke to me about how fragile and precious my girl's hearts and spirits are to Him. Our children are sensitive and what we say and do forever impacts them. Colossians 3:21 (NLT) says, "Fathers, do not aggravate your children, or they will become discouraged." With this kind of behavior over time, we can truly break our children's hearts and spirits. Our children do not need a rigid taskmaster but a loving encourager!

Dear mama, I have learned that we as mothers need to truly become students of our children. We need to ask the Lord how to best love them, challenge them, and teach them. And each one of our kids is so different. Now, let me assure you that I am no expert and this was not an immediate change. Raising my voice is still something I struggle with, but I have matured in my faith and I have openly discussed this with my husband so he can help keep me accountable. This refining process was oh so important for me, as I often like to pretend that I have no issues in my mothering.

As parents, my husband and I have continually discussed how much power and responsibility we have to nurture our children's hearts. However, after said child has done something that frustrates us, our tendency is to lose our temper and say something we regret. This is a dangerous and slippery slope! With every sharply delivered word or disapproving stare, our children's hearts become smaller and more hidden away. Our children need a mom who trusts in the Lord with all her heart and leans not on her own understanding (Proverbs 3:5). Our precious children deserve a mama who can remain calm and gain her strength from her heavenly Father.

I would like to encourage you, dearest mama, to avoid overreacting to minor child mishaps and accidents. If there is a legitimate issue with your child that does need to be addressed, I encourage you to lead by example. Show your child that you can remain calm. Also, model for your child the most important thing: turning to Jesus in prayer and reading His Word. Let them know that mommy has to ask God for help too and that you're not perfect. They will appreciate not feeling like they are the only ones who mess up. Let's all celebrate our children by nurturing and protecting their hearts together!

FAITH-FILLED IDEA: Catch Them Being Good

Let's focus on praising our wonderful children by "catching them being good." This is such a fun activity that your children will really appreciate! Create a joy jar that is simple and easy. When your child does something sweet for their sibling or does something for you without being told, let them put a marble in the joy jar. When the joy jar is full, take them out for ice cream!

Go even further and make lists for all your children celebrating the qualities and talents you love and admire about them. Read the list out loud (or have your husband read it) to all your children over dinner one night. Their little hearts will swell with encouragement.

26

Speak Life to Your Children

DEB WEAKLY

*God...gives life to the dead and speaks of
things that don't yet exist as if they are real.*

Romans 4:17 ERV

*You may speak but a word to a child, and in that
child, there may be slumbering a noble heart which
shall stir the Christian Church in years to come.*

Charles Spurgeon

My kids never quite fit into any mold. As a matter of fact, I had the ones (particularly one) that would always get into trouble everywhere we went. I was usually the mom leaving the playgroup with a crying child and who felt discouraged and sad because going places with this child was so hard! My Christie was the one who constantly had to touch every little thing she saw. She frequently had her little toe right on the edge of the line that you told her not to cross. And to make matters worse, she possessed more energy than any other child I had ever known, and this energy kept going and going until the very last moment when we put her to bed at night. Oh, I'm still tired just thinking about it!

But you know what I learned? God made Christie hugely curious, not the normal curious but the curious that constantly wanted to learn and engage her brain. The only problem is that sometimes it came across as disobedience because I could rarely keep up with her. She appeared to frequently challenge me, when in reality, she just wanted to keep going, learning more, and was rarely content to sit on her laurels. She needed constant activity and stimulation for her little growing brain. The world would label her strong-willed, and I was often exasperated in trying to control her. Oh, how I wish I would have understood her better when she was little and given her more grace and patience.

My mama heart prayed for my little girl, and I cried out to God day and night for help and wisdom. During this time, my husband was reading *The Sacred Romance* by John Eldredge. Through this book, he became aware of the power of focusing on the good in people and seeing them as they could become, not as they presently are. We both agreed to apply this principle of speaking of things that don't yet exist as if they are real (Romans 4:17 ERV) to our daughter. Our words have power and can show our faith or lack of it. My daughter was not well behaved all the time, but we began to treat Christie like she was the sweet, godly, purpose-driven person she could become. I believe this one habit changed our relationships with our daughter and set the stage for the beautiful, close relationship we all enjoy as a family now.

Thankfully, God gave my husband and me wisdom each day to know how to change our old habits and speak "life" into our children. He gave us the strength, patience, and perseverance we needed to raise up our children for Him, and He can give you everything you need to be the best parents for your children too. Pray daily for your children and for you and your husband to see their hearts and accept them the way God made them. If speaking kind, edifying words doesn't come naturally to you, ask God for the words to say to build them up. Lean into your heavenly Father and try to give grace as much as possible.

Start to speak life to your children as much as possible, even in the little things. Say things like "You are so kind! That was so sweet of you to let your sister have the big chair" or "You are so trustworthy! Thank you for waiting for Mommy to help you cross the street." When your child makes a mistake, call their attention to it, discipline them as quickly as possible, and move on. Don't drag out your discipline! Take care of things before Daddy gets home. Don't make poor Dad come home to a house of turmoil and stress. Lastly, let your children know you forgive them and that Mommy and Daddy make lots of mistakes too. Most people, including children, will rise to what's expected of them.

Oh, and if you happen to have a Christie, take heart. They are wonderful blessings! My Christie is now happily married to an amazing, godly man, and they both love Jesus with their whole hearts. She graduated with a computer science degree, devours several books at a time, and is still curious and loves to learn. She is also a patient, attentive, and kind-hearted mom.

I have decided that I am so happy my children didn't fit the mold. Life is just so much more interesting this way!

FAITH-FILLED IDEA: Pick a Hymn for Your Child

Do you have a difficult child? Instead of complaining about him or her to your friends, pray instead. Ask God to give you a list of encouraging words you can speak over each child. Write them in your journal and use them to "call forth" the possibilities in your child's life or your situation. Pick a hymn for your child and sing it to them. Frame it and hang it in their room as a special declaration. Go to page 202 for instructions on "Picking a Hymn for Your Child."

27

Holding On to God's Promises for Your Special-Needs Child

BRANDI CARSON

Love is patient and kind; love does not envy or boast; it is not arrogant or rude. It does not insist on its own way; it is not irritable or resentful.

1 Corinthians 13:4-5 ESV

What gives me the most hope every day is God's grace; knowing that his grace is going to give me the strength for whatever I face, knowing that nothing is a surprise to God.

Rick Warren

Being a mama is hard work. Being a mama to a special-needs child or a child with a physical disability is tremendously hard work. As a mother, you can read all the books, choose to homeschool or choose to put your child in a specialized public school that caters to their strengths, and go to all the counselors and doctors. You can also figure out and show all the love languages and spend the quality time, and sometimes, life at home is still incredibly difficult. When you first set eyes on that precious newborn baby, and you took your first breath of that sweet baby smell, the thought never crossed your mind that your child would someday struggle through life with mental illness and/or special needs. Just when you think the calm is near, another wave comes crashing on top of you, leaving you disoriented and not knowing where to turn next.

This is my life—my daily struggle. It is overwhelming. It is exhausting. It is harder than anything I could have ever imagined life could be. It has taught me to fight fiercely, love unconditionally, live sacrificially, let go of expectations, dig in deeply, and persevere endlessly. It has made me strong. It has made me faithful. It has taught me more about myself than I ever expected to know and made me a better version of myself, all the while clinging tightly to the promises God spoke to me years ago about my sweet girl. You see, dear mama, God knows my daughter and loves her unconditionally. That promise keeps me going!

My friend, I am here to give you hope. This journey has been hard, and it is not over. If you have a difficult child or a child with special needs, physical or mental, I am here to tell you not to give up. There are hard times, dark times, trying times, but praise Jesus, He also brings times of redemption, times of victory, and times of success. Having a child like this can bring you to the end of yourself, but that is where God is waiting for you. He *never* leaves you and *never* forsakes you. Lean on Him, seek Him, pray to Him, and ask for guidance, direction, and supernatural peace. When you are too tired and worn out and don't feel like you can pray anymore, ask those closest to you to pray with and for you and your child and your family. This is a battle you don't have to do alone! A verse that I often cling to is James 1:12, "Blessed is the one who perseveres under trial because, having stood the test, that person will receive the crown of life that the Lord has promised to those who love him."

Several years ago, I started praying fiercely for my daughter and began asking God to show me how He saw her. He responded by revealing to me powerful imagery of a strong woman full of the Holy Spirit with so much to offer the world. He showed me my daughter's beauty and strength and how she is going to do so much for His kingdom. When things are hard with her and I begin to feel hopeless, I cling tightly to those images and His promises!

If you are in a place with your child where you are feeling hopeless, pray. Ask God to show you who your child is in His eyes and who He created them to be. Ask Him to give you a promise or a specific Scripture for your child, so in those moments of darkness, when you feel that there is no light, you have something to hold on to. Seek His truth, and do not listen to the world. Dear friend, know, with all certainty, that God made *you* the perfect mom for your child! You are capable, beautiful, and cherished.

FAITH-FILLED IDEA: Pray Scripture Out Loud

Praying Scripture out loud over your child is just one way to show them you love them. It is a powerful and tangible way to cover your child who is going through a hard time. For a list of prayers, check out page 202.

28

Parenting with Grace

MARI JO MAST

*Do not provoke your children to anger by the way
you treat them. Rather, bring them up with the
discipline and instruction that comes from the Lord.*

Ephesians 6:4 NLT

*You are not in this parenting drama alone. Your
potential is greater than the size of your weaknesses,
because the One who is without weakness is with you,
and he does his best work through those who admit
that they are weak but in weakness still heed his call.*

Paul David Trip

Dear mama, years ago when my children were much younger, I struggled to keep up with them. Ah, they required so much of my time and attention, plus they were naughty (like, a lot)! I felt embarrassed when they misbehaved, because it often happened while we were with friends or out in public. Motivated out of pride, I tried to stop and control their bad behavior. Have you ever felt exasperated as a mom, like me?

Motherhood became more difficult when a well-meaning mom offered me advice—to discipline my children *every* time they disobeyed, talked back, or displayed a wrong attitude. It was explained, if I failed to punish every single time, it would allow rebellion to run rampant in our home. I was overwhelmed because we had five children at the time, and you can imagine how impossible it was to correct every time. Words of frustration continually came out of my mouth because I was exhausted!

Dear sister, it grieves my heart as I remember: I became a policeman in my own home. I "arrested" the kids all day long, disciplining them for their every "crime." I thought I had to force them into submission somehow, so I kept track of all the naughty things they did.

Please know my policing didn't work but only strengthened sin even more! I didn't realize it at the time, but when all you do is focus on punishing bad behavior, that's what happens.

What if God always watched and punished us for every wrong we did? I'm pretty sure I wouldn't still be alive!

Oh, friend, what my children needed was more of Jesus—to be discipled in His truth, with words of life and blessing spoken over them. I needed godly vision to see their hearts and to minister genuine kindness and loving instruction to them—a love that showed pure enjoyment in our relationship, one that cherished and nurtured their tender hearts, just as Jesus daily exemplified to me.

It's hard to live a life of servanthood and be an example of patience when our children act naughty. Oh, how I wish that in this difficult season, I would have consistently and calmly demonstrated to my children that I would always love and accept them, no matter how badly they behaved. My example could have assured them that God loved and accepted them too. All children need this assurance. Their behavior is only a by-product of a much greater need—to have a relationship with Jesus. As mothers, we can help pull them out of their sin and lead them to the one who bore all their sin (Jesus).

Parenting like Jesus won't bring "instant" holiness. Instead, it takes lots and lots of time and commitment—it takes repentance and the Holy Spirit.

Dear one, please be careful who you listen to. When we become overwhelmed and desperate, we do and say crazy things we regret later. Our children are precious—created with dignity and made in the image of God. We will give an account some day of how we steward our children.

God revealed to Solomon a long, long time ago that the words we speak have a profound effect on everything and everyone around us. Proverbs 18:21-22 (KJV) says, "A man's belly shall be satisfied with the fruit of his mouth; and with the increase of his lips shall he be filled. Death and life are in the power of the tongue: and they that love it shall eat the fruit thereof."

Death and life result in what we speak—take a moment to think about that!

It's sobering to realize our homes over time become a product of what we consistently think and say to our children. Our speaking habits create the path our children walk on while they live with us. We play such a large part in shaping them into what they believe about themselves, and they will carry that identity with them for a long time.

It's never too late to love our children unconditionally, like God loves us. I'm so thankful for His grace and mercy! Life-giving words spoken while we disciple them will transform their lives. Our past failures don't define our children when we repent and turn to the Lord.

Mama, I really wish I could sit down and pray words of life over you. Maybe as a child you experienced a lot of pain because of the words spoken over you by a parent. I want you to know God loves you and wants to heal your heart. God helps us parent better than we were raised!

I pray the Holy Spirit brings supernatural healing to any brokenness and pain from your past. May you experience His sweet healing, like oil poured over a deep wound, bringing an understanding of His never-ending love. I pray you surrender and experience it from the depths of your very being. You are created for true love too—it begins with you.

FAITH-FILLED IDEA: Use the Six Powerful Keys

Check the "HELPful Resources" on page 203 for "The Powerful Six List," which helps me parent with more grace. I hope it will encourage you in your mothering journey! It is simple yet profound, and all of it comes from God's Word. His wisdom is far greater than ours and so practical. Truly His ways are genius and life changing!

"I have loved you with an everlasting love; I have drawn you with unfailing kindness" (Jeremiah 31:3).

29

The Ministry of a Christian Stepmom

······· DEB WEAKLY ·······

*Make my joy complete by being like-minded, having
the same love, being one in spirit and of one mind.
Do nothing out of selfish ambition or vain conceit.
Rather, in humility value others above yourselves, not
looking to your own interests but each of you to the
interests of the others. In your relationships with one
another, have the same mindset as Christ Jesus.*

Philippians 2:2-5

*All that I am or ever hope to be,
I owe to my angel mother.*

Abraham Lincoln—of his stepmother, Sarah.

Mothers are important; we mold the hearts and minds of the next generation. The importance is not only true of birth and adoptive moms but also stepmoms.

My parents divorced when I was young, and my dad remarried. Daddy had full custody of me, so I lived with him and my stepmom full-time. These short years became one of the most difficult seasons of my life. My parents' recent divorce left me feeling wounded and broken. Furthermore, my stepmom didn't want me, so I never felt loved and accepted living in her home. They divorced a short time later, and I felt relieved.

After their divorce, my dad dated a delightful woman named Sharon. Though they never married and were only together a short time, I will always remember Sharon for the way she loved me like a daughter and taught me much about life. She helped me learn all about how to apply cosmetics and hosted my friends for sleepovers. Sharon was a delightful cook and loved to decorate. She was a beautiful example of a sweet mother-figure who chose to invest her life into a defeated young girl.

My dad later married a kind woman named Jean. My children know Jean as Nanny, and she loves them like her own grandchildren. Jean was just what I needed as an adult stepchild. She loved my dad well and took care of him until the end of his life. I will always be thankful for my sweet stepmom, Jean.

As a stepmom, you have the God-given potential to make an enormous difference in the lives of your stepchildren. I fervently believe this is a ministry given to you by God to show His love to your potentially wounded stepchildren and teens.

I don't know your situation. The children's birth mom may be fantastic, and if so, the children are blessed to have her. Much of the time, however, the mom may have deep wounds, which make it hard for her to be the mother her children need. In any case, don't ever underestimate the power of your ministry to your stepchildren. You will never replace their mom, but you can be a positive role model and someone who is always there for them and shows them the love of Jesus.

While praying over this article, I thought about the things I needed from my stepmoms when I was living with them. I felt the Lord impressing on me to discuss five practical ways you can love your stepchildren during this season with your blended family in your home:

1. Pray! Prayer is your greatest work in your home. Pray for your husband and stepchildren to feel the love of Jesus in your home through you. Don't forget to pray for the children's birth mom and for healing to take place in her heart as well. Prayer changes everything!

2. Be patient and keep loving, no matter what. The children may resent you, but know they are hurting during this difficult season. Ask God to help you love supernaturally with the love of Christ.

3. Cook as much as possible! Break out your Crock-Pot and make sure the children have delicious smells in the kitchen when they come home. Have dinners together as much as you can, even if you are all busy!

4. Be present, be available, and listen. Be there! Try to be home when the children are home. Take the time to ask about their day and listen. Give lots of sweet hugs. Go to their sporting practices and events. Host their friends in your home for special dinners and sleepovers. Your relationship will take a significant investment of time, but it's worth it!

5. Stay positive as much as possible. Don't ever vent about their mom, your husband, or any situation to the children. Let them be children. They most likely have gone through a lot of difficulties with their parents' divorce and have wounds of their own. I lost my childhood and had to grow up fast because of my parents' divorce; they probably have too. They need time and prayers to heal. The Lord will help them!

FAITH-FILLED IDEA: Make Time for Table Talk

Prayerfully plan time this week for meals together around the table at home. Make a weekend night special by making dinner together. Try our "Homemade Pizza Dough" recipe on page 207. Be intentional about really listening to your stepkids as they talk during dinner. Ask the question, "What's the best thing that happened to you today?" or "High/Low?" (What's your highlight for the day, and what is one challenging situation?). These dinner conversations will help you to stay connected with your kids and know what is going on in their hearts.

30

Let Them Do It Their Way!

······· RACHEL JONES ·······

*Listen, my son, to your father's instruction and do not
forsake your mother's teaching. They are a garland
to grace your head and a chain to adorn your neck.*

Proverbs 1:8-9

*Tell me and I forget, teach me and I may
remember, involve me and I will learn.*

Benjamin Franklin

I am the type of mother who would rather do the household chore, cook the dinner, and bake the muffins by myself because it is easier but also because I am slightly a control freak. Being a mother has stretched me so much, and I still struggle a lot. I love my children tremendously and yearn to sit back and watch them grow by learning to do things themselves. However, involving my kids can often be messy, annoying, and actually cause many things to take longer than necessary. Do you agree with me, mama?

Deep down in my heart though, I know this way of thinking and approaching responsibilities is wrong. Friends, I have been convicted, and I want to share with you what the Lord has taught me: We need to allow our children to learn by our gentle instruction, even when it is hard to submit control. When we let our children do it their way, it shows them that God loves them exactly where they're at. It also gives them an immense amount of satisfaction. Most children will mess up in

116

the beginning; however, teaching them is what we are called to do, and we are equipping them to be more capable human beings in the process.

Ephesians 6:4 says we are to "bring [our children] up in the training and instruction of the Lord." As mothers, the Lord has called us to train up our children. This is essential and there is no gray area here! During the process of training and teaching, our relationship with our children grows. We begin to walk beside them and can witness firsthand the ways in which the Lord is growing them and drawing them closer to Him.

The Lord has spoken to me time and time again about this, and my prayer is that I can change my ways and encourage you, mama, to do the same. As mothers, we need to take the time to show our children how to do the dishes, fold their laundry, and empty the trash. We need to consistently allow them to mess up and still praise their efforts, even if they are doing the job in a less than perfect way, because it is their way. We need to also gently nudge them to take responsibility for their homework and other school projects.

Another important aspect of teaching our children more responsibilities is training them to have a good attitude while completing the task. While working on jobs around the house ourselves, we need to do them with a joyful and grateful heart. Ultimately, our children strive to be like us, and they are always watching with their curious eyes. Don't we want them to see a mama who is thankful she has floors to clean and trash to collect? Children tend to do their chores begrudgingly: Let's endeavor to show them not only how to finish a job but how it can be done in good spirits as well!

After all, we eventually want our children to accept ownership for a task or chore and to do it without being told. Our prayer is that our children will do the job because it needs to be done and accept that it is their obligation to do it. This is called teaching our children responsibility in love! We need to model Proverbs 22:6 and "train up a child in the way he should go" (KJV). This is the will of God for us as parents, and how much does He love us even in our mess? Children see what is happening and they watch our every move. Perfection is not possible.

By allowing our children to "do it their way," we are championing a feeling of pride, accomplishment, and joy in their little hearts.

In the end, accountability, responsibility, and obedience are what the Lord demands of our children, and we have the honor to model and teach them these qualities. We will be doing our children a huge disservice if we don't rise to this vital occasion. Over time, I have observed a beautiful principle—the children most accountable to act responsibly are the happiest and most secure in love and grounded in goodwill—in His goodwill.

FAITH-FILLED IDEA: Give Them a Job

Okay, mama! I am so honored to encourage and nudge you in the right direction toward training your children. I have compiled a list of simple jobs for different age groups. Use it! Accept this challenge and change the way your household is run. Refer to the "HELPful Resources" on page 204.

31

Having Fun with Your Kids

KRYSTLE PORTER

I concluded there is nothing better than to be happy and enjoy ourselves as long as we can. And people should eat and drink and enjoy the fruits of their labor, for these are gifts from God.

Ecclesiastes 3:12-13 NLT

If you want your children to be intelligent, read them fairy tales. If you want them to be more intelligent, read them more fairy tales.

Albert Einstein

On a normal school night, my family can be caught having a dinner dance party outside on our patio. We turn on our string lights that cover our picnic table and put on a mix of different types of music while rotating turns taking center stage. We all lively clap for each other and pretend the person performing is the most amazing of all time!

The idea of having fun with our kids can overwhelm us sometimes. After all, kids can tend to make life more complicated than it needs to be. Can I get an amen? Planning something fun, like heading to a park (or anywhere for that matter), can be full of frustrations. One child can't find their shoes, another needs to go to the bathroom just as buckles are being fastened in the car, someone needs a snack, the baby is crying and needs a diaper change, or there are just bad attitudes all around. Just writing all that out makes me feel like staying home!

So why be intentional in having fun with our kids? Because God gave us our sweet kids not just to manage and take care of their needs but to delight in them! One tip that I like to give fellow moms is to plan just one fun thing to do with your kids per day. It is unrealistic to *always* have an entire day devoted to frivolity and fun. But one sweet surprise in your child's day can sure make them light up, no matter what age! Don't go crazy planning. Kids seriously appreciate even our smallest efforts to seek them out and enjoy one another.

Life is full of mundane tasks and chores. If we aren't careful, the mundane can take over life. Though I don't think that's what God had in mind for us when He created this masterpiece called earth. As I search the skies and landscapes God created for His people, I am continually convinced that God intended for us to not just live life but to stop and enjoy it, both in the beauty of the universe and inside our homes that He has given us. I think about the ocean and the creatures He put in its vastness—all for our amazement and His glory! Or the power of a rainstorm and the sweet smell of rain when it is all through, making the world clean again. God intended us to marvel at His handiwork.

This makes me think of the miracle that is our children. When that precious baby is laid on your chest for the first time and the world stops. How can you even love a single person on the planet as much as this small, fragile soul you just met? You don't even know them yet, but you are awestruck with inexplicable delight. Friends, that is God's gift of enjoyment on this earth. Little snippets of heaven that we get to experience here and now. It is the fun and delight that balances out our struggles of this life.

Recently, all five of my children were sick. We were quarantined to our home for weeks upon weeks. We all were in a rut and desperately needed some fun in our lives. Remember the dinner dance party I mentioned above? That was during this specific time, and we repeated that fun multiple times! We made some time for read-aloud stories and milk and cookies. We took a long bike ride where it rained on us, and we picked oranges off trees for an unexpected treat when we got lost along the way. The point is, fun isn't only fun when life is all sunshine and roses. There is fun to be had all along the way. Fun can be simple or extravagant. Never feel like what you have to work with isn't good enough. Dance parties in the living room with hairbrush microphones are absolutely free!

Also, each and every day can be redeemed by fun. If you've had a bad day, light a few candles, put on some music, and make some cinnamon-sugar toast. Watch as smiles light up your table and conversations start to flow!

Do you find yourself or your family in a season where you need a little more enjoyment of this intricate and beautiful world that God placed you in? Seize the day. And seize it again tomorrow! You will remember all the memories you make for years to come, and your kids will too.

FAITH-FILLED IDEA: Twenty-Five Fun Activities

Every mom needs to let loose occasionally and have fun with her children! For a list of twenty-five great activities to do with your kids, see page 205 in the "HELPful Resources."

32

Drawing Our Children Close

· · · · · · · · · · · · · · · · · · · TARA DAVIS · · · · · · · · · · · · · · · · · · ·

Children are a gift from the LORD;
they are a reward from him.

Psalm 127:3 NLT

Motherhood is a million little moments that
God weaves together with grace, redemption,
laughter, tears, and most of all love. Such a gift.

Lysa TerKeurst

I sat in an old, worn armchair feeding my third baby as I watched the early morning light filtering through pine trees outside our window. It was so beautiful, but I was so tired. I couldn't seem to manage all that I felt was expected of me and my frustration with life was just one situation away from spilling out of my soul in a hot mess of emotion. Oh, how I wanted some peace and quiet and maybe even a little bit of order. I wanted everyone to just go away for a little while, to quit being so loud, to quit needing me so much.

I looked down at my little one's pudgy, dimpled baby hands and glanced over at my two wonderful, growing boys wrestling on the floor, and a wave of guilt flashed like lightning across my mind. How many times had I, in my exhaustion and frustration, pushed them away? How many times had I chosen the path of "not now" or "I'm too busy" instead of embracing their littleness, enjoying their wildness, and jumping feet first into the messy "yes" of intentional mothering?

My dear friend, some days the temper tantrums, squabbles, and diapers seem never-ending, don't they? You so desperately want to do this mom-thing right. Me too. When my older boys were still babies, I looked everywhere for examples of godly moms to follow. I just wanted someone to tell me exactly what to do to make this all work out. I just wanted these wild ones of mine to turn out okay in the end. But with all that searching and fretting and wishing, I should have just looked up to the Lord.

Oh, how our Father loves us. Isaiah 40:11 says, "He tends his flock like a shepherd: He gathers the lambs in his arms and carries them close to his heart; he gently leads those that have young." He's talking about us right there, my friend. He gently leads us moms with little (and big) lambs of our own. All we need to do is follow Him as we embrace these children He has gifted to us!

And oh, how I want to be a parent like my Father! In Hosea 11:4, God speaks lovingly of His children Israel, saying, "I led them with cords of human kindness, with ties of love. To them I was like one who lifts a little child to the cheek, and I bent down to feed them." God's gentle love for His children, the way He draws them with kindness and lifts their burdens is beautiful, isn't it? It almost sounds like Israel is an easy child. But all we need to do is glance through the first few books of the Bible to see that Israel was a disobedient, defiant disaster. Yet our Father still loved them. Instead of pushing them away, He gently drew His children close to Himself.

God continually meets His children where they are, lifting them up during hardships, shouldering their burdens, and pouring His life-changing love into their hearts. Oh, what sweet grace to be able to follow the Lord's example with our own children! But what about the times when we are exhausted, disappointed, frustrated, and overwhelmed?

In Colossians 3:12, we can find God's truth for these times, "Therefore, as God's chosen people, holy and dearly loved, clothe yourselves with compassion, kindness, humility, gentleness and patience." There it is. When we are tired, when our children misbehave, when we have to break up yet another sibling fight, and when it seems they will just never listen, we are to allow the Lord to clothe us with compassion, kindness, humility, gentleness, and patience. We are to follow our

Father's example and pick up our children, draw them to our heart with tenderness, and show them the gentleness of the Lord in our words and actions as we shoulder their burdens.

And with our children pulled close to our heart, we are able to say yes to their exuberance for life. Yes to the thousand questions they ask, yes to the sticky hand in ours, yes to kneeling at their level and teaching their heart when they are disobedient, yes to rocking them to sleep on tear-soaked nights, yes to speaking truth in a kind tone, yes to living ourselves the way we have asked them to live, and yes to walking the path of Christ's love one day at a time.

Let's love these loud, crazy, beautiful children of ours just as Jesus does; we have them with us for such a short while. Our lives will one day be cleaner and less chaotic, and we won't feel so much like we are on the verge of losing our minds, but our sweetest ones will be grown. Will you choose to love this time with them and draw them tenderly to your heart even when you feel like pulling away? With God all things are possible, mama!

FAITH-FILLED IDEA: Have a Time-In

It is so easy to push our kids away, especially in times of frustration. Consider having a time-in when your child is upset instead of a time-out. Let them climb into a chair with you and talk with them about how to calm down, take deep breaths, and think on good things as the Bible instructs us in Philippians 4:8. Pray with your child that God will help them with their struggles and will create within them a clean heart. Use this time to teach your child how to run to God for help and comfort.

Scriptures to Pray for Your Children

Pray that your children will follow the Lord with their whole heart and serve Him their whole life.

> "It is the LORD your God you must follow, and him you must revere. Keep his commands and obey him; serve him and hold fast to him" (Deuteronomy 13:4).

Pray that your children will be strong and courageous as they face the challenges before them.

> "Have I not commanded you? Be strong and courageous. Do not be afraid; do not be discouraged, for the LORD your God will be with you wherever you go" (Joshua 1:9).

Pray that they will be powerful leaders in speech, in action, in love, in faith, and in purity.

> "Don't let anyone look down on you because you are young, but set an example for the believers in speech, in conduct, in love, in faith and in purity" (1 Timothy 4:12).

Pray that your children will know they can do all things through God's strength.

> "I can do all this through him who gives me strength" (Philippians 4:13).

Pray that your children will become hard workers, to please God alone.

> "Whatever you do, work at it with all your heart, as working for the Lord, not for human masters" (Colossians 3:23).

Pray that they will shine the light of Jesus each day so that others will see the goodness of God.

> "In the same way, let your light shine before others, that they may see your good deeds and glorify your Father in heaven" (Matthew 5:16).

Pray that your children will stand apart in this world by doing the will of God and following Him.

> "Do not conform to the pattern of this world, but be transformed by the renewing of your mind. Then you will be able to test and approve what God's will is—his good, pleasing and perfect will" (Romans 12:2).

Pray that God will open your children's eyes to His purpose and plans for their lives.

> "For we are God's handiwork, created in Christ Jesus to do good works, which God prepared in advance for us to do" (Ephesians 2:10).

Pray that your children will be kind, compassionate, and forgiving toward others.

> "Be kind and compassionate to one another, forgiving each other, just as in Christ God forgave you" (Ephesians 4:32).

Pray that they will know the unfailing love of God and take refuge in Him.

> "How priceless is your unfailing love, O God! People take refuge in the shadow of your wings" (Psalm 36:7).

Part 4

The Wise Woman Creates a Home

Sweet one, your homemaking matters. All the meals you cook, snacks you provide, every bit of cleaning you do, and anything else you do in your home with love makes a difference for all eternity. God cares about every tiny way you care for your family, and He is so pleased by your love. Your labor is not in vain.

The Bible doesn't contain many instructions specific to women, but Titus 2:5 says that we are to be "homemakers." It's a compound word with big potential. When you look well to the ways of your household and the people in it, whether you're at work all day, stay at home, or somewhere in between, you are just like a conductor who creates the greatest symphony of her life—your magnum opus.

As women, we hear many messages on the subject of homemaking, and we all want to make our homes perfect. But what if we go to God and ask Him how He wants our houses to look and feel instead of comparing ourselves with other moms we know. It's okay—in fact, it's good—if your home is unique to you and your family. We're here to say this: The space under your roof doesn't need to be picture perfect.

Biblical homemaking is more about the ministry that takes place between your walls, the meals you share, the space you provide for your children and their friends to rest and play and laugh. Your home should be clean enough to where it doesn't drive you crazy but messy enough to where your kids aren't afraid to have fun, discover, and create. As you go through the articles in this section, pray and ask God to show you any changes He may want you to make in your heart or in your home. And remember, "You do you!" Your home life will not look exactly like any of ours, and that's so good. God loves variety!

love, Deb

33

Establishing a Life-Giving Routine in Your Home

.... DEB WEAKLY ....

*She watches over the affairs of her household
and does not eat the bread of idleness. Her
children arise and call her blessed; her husband
also, and he praises her: "Many women do
noble things, but you surpass them all."*

Proverbs 31:27-29

*The habits of the child produce
the character of the man.*

Charlotte Mason

Once upon a time, I was a mom with littles. I remember how much fun it was to have young children in my home, but it was also exhausting. I remember days when I would be home all day, but nothing actually got done. As a young mom, I knew I needed to have some structure to my day so I could use my best hours spending time with my children while the homemaking duties still got accomplished. Now as an empty-nester, I feel the Lord guiding me toward sharing about a life-giving routine that leads to a more peaceful and joy-filled home. When I speak of a life-giving routine, I do not mean a rigid schedule. The type of routine I am talking about is more like a rhythm. A rhythm feels peaceful, not controlling. It allows for illnesses or a friend coming over to play. When we rule over our schedule instead of allowing our schedule to rule over us, we can enjoy spur-of-the-moment fun activities, knowing that the schedule will return to normal in a day or two. A rhythm helps you enjoy your life and the moments God brings across your path. It also helps your children feel safe and secure when they know what comes next.

Here are a few tips for your family on how to establish a life-giving routine in your home:

Mornings in your home should be pleasant. Greeting your children with a smile and telling them you are glad to see them creates a joy-filled start for their day. Put worship music on in their rooms as you wake them up and tell them, "This *is* the day the LORD has made. We will rejoice and be glad in it" (Psalm 118:24 NKJV). Help your children learn to love mornings from a young age.

To help your mornings go more smoothly, set the breakfast table the night before. Make sure you have what you need to enjoy a simple meal together. Be sure to pray with your children for their day and read a little devotion from a children's Bible. It's a great way to start the day!

After breakfast, while driving to school or other activities, listen to a fun CD of kids' worship. We made it a point to only listen to children's worship music or books on tape in the car when we drove with the kids. When we dropped them off at any activity, we would tell them to "Go M.A.D!" meaning "Go Make A Difference!" Doing this helped our kids be mindful that they could make a difference for the kingdom of God, no matter their age.

Have quiet time in the afternoon. When our children grew out of their naps, we gave them the choice to sleep, read, or listen to a book on tape in their rooms for an hour while I rested in my room. Our daughter now says that these were some of her best times and that she loved that hour of resting and reading great books. Our son would quietly play with Legos in his room and listen to *Adventures in Odyssey*.

Make family dinners a priority. Establish a time for regular family dinners with no TV. Carve out time to eat together, even if you have sports or other activities, and make sure to ask each other questions. In our home, we always asked the question, "What's the best thing that happened to you today?" or "High/Low?" which meant, "What was the best part of your day, and what was the most challenging part of your day?" These questions helped us connect with one another and to linger at the table a little while longer. The dinner hour should be a sweet memory for your children. When dinner is over, everyone helps pick up and clean. Put on some fun, active music and dance around the kitchen together as you clean.

Create a fun bedtime routine for your children! Be sure to begin bath time and bedtime early enough to where you can take your time putting your children to bed. The bedtime hour should be one associated with a sweetness of spending time with Mom and Dad. In our home, we read books to our kids at night. Randy even read science encyclopedias filled with pictures to our daughter, Christie. As a child, science was her passion, and she is now happily employed as a software engineer. They also read through all the C.S. Lewis children's books.

Let your kids listen to fun books on tape after you tuck them in. You will need to account for this in your bedtime routine. We put our kids to bed twenty minutes earlier so they could listen to their favorite audiobook. To access a great list of our favorite audiobooks, please go to myhelpclubformoms.com.

Don't sign your kids up for too many activities! One per child is plenty. Resist the urge to schedule every moment of your child's life. Trust me, it's not worth it. A child needs time to simply be a child.

. . . .

FAITH-FILLED IDEA:
Making Sunday Mornings Special

. . . .

Do your kids dread Sunday morning because of the craziness of simply trying to get to church on time? Take a cue from Jewish moms who begin getting ready for the Sabbath several days before the day of worship arrives: Start preparing for Sunday morning on Friday! Make sure you have food in the fridge for a special Sunday breakfast. In our house, I always made a big breakfast on Sunday with bacon and pancakes. The delicious smells always helped get my kids out of bed with a good attitude! Be sure to lay out their clothes and everything they need for church on Saturday night, including their Bible and tithe. Gas up your car on Friday so you are ready to go! Pray with your kids on the way to church. Be sure to hang around after church is over to chat with friends and maybe even take one of your kids' best buds out to lunch with you. They will love these memories of fun Sundays in their home!

34

Spirit-Filled Homemaking

····················· RACHEL JONES ·····················

> *By wisdom a house is built, and through understanding it is established; through knowledge its rooms are filled with rare and beautiful treasures.*
>
> **Proverbs 24:3-4**

> *What you do in your house is worth as much as if you did it up in heaven for our Lord God. We should accustom ourselves to think of our position and work as sacred and well-pleasing to God, not on account of the position and work, but on account of the word and faith from which the obedience and the work flow.*
>
> **Martin Luther**

Whether you work outside the home or stay home full-time, you are a homemaker. All women have been called by God to make the place where their family lives a home. Making our house a home is hard work, and I am currently in the trenches with you ladies. My days are mostly spent in the kitchen and laundry room; I swear my children never stop eating or making messes! I am so blessed to be home full-time with four kiddos under the age of eleven, but it was not always this way.

A few years ago, before we had our fourth, I worked part-time outside of the house. I remember feeling behind in my housework constantly, and I felt so bad when I could not complete the "extras," such as having warm banana bread on the counter at all times or organizing every closet by style and color. But why was I feeling bad? My husband didn't care, and I was putting so much unnecessary guilt on myself that it took away from my happiness when I was home.

I am so thankful for that season because it gave me such great perspective on homemaking. Dear mama, homemaking is so much more than cleaning a house, cooking food, and making sure our family has clothes to wear. Homemaking is about nurturing a spirit of warmth, comfort, and love in our homes. As the book of Proverbs says, "She looks well to the ways of her household and does not eat the bread of idleness" (31:27 ESV). We all need to "look well" to our homes and feel amazing pride when we think of them. What brings me comfort and fills my heart with peace and contentment regarding my home is the Holy Spirit. Without His presence, I would be floundering without purpose or direction.

One of my favorite Bible verses is 2 Timothy 1:7 (NLT): "For God has not given us a spirit of fear and timidity, but of *power, love,* and *self-discipline.*" We are all talented women of God who have the *power* to do what is right for our home. Dear mama, we have unconditional *love* from the Holy Spirit to care for our family. And within all of us is the *self-discipline* to keep our hearts and minds focused on God and to have Him at the center of our household.

A woman's spirit affects her whole house. We all have the power to instill peace, love, and joy in our homes. We also have the amazing opportunity to encourage our husbands and children to become closer to the Lord. What we say is extremely influential, and our moods can dramatically affect the flow of the home. Proverbs 21:9 (ISV) says, "It's better to live in a corner on the roof than to share a house with a contentious woman." Wow! I do not want my husband or kids to ever feel that they would rather live in a corner on the roof than in my home, and I am sure you would all agree with me. It would break my heart! However, all too often, I lose my temper or challenge my husband in front of our kids, which absolutely destroys the peacefulness of our home.

My prayer for you is to see the incredible honor it is to have a home. God has gifted you with one of His best blessings—a family to love and care for and to guide toward Him. During those especially exhausting moments, simply look at your kids. By truly looking at those beautiful children, who cherish every moment in their mama's presence, you will quickly be reminded of what's important. Focus less on *what* is on the table and more on *who* is around the table. Focus on the legacy you hope to leave. That legacy starts today with your mind set on the Lord!

Every household is so vastly different. Do not look to others and make comparisons. Put your blinders on, and you do you! You are the best wife for your husband, and you are the best mom for your children.

FAITH-FILLED IDEA: Help with Your Laundry

Every home produces tons of dirty laundry, and we are here to help! Let us come alongside you and make doing laundry a little bit more fun and save you money at the same time. An amazing "Homemade Laundry Detergent" recipe is on page 210 in the "HELPful Resources."

35

"Choosing What Is Better" in Our Homes

KRYSTLE PORTER

"Martha, Martha," the Lord answered, "you are worried and upset about many things, but few things are needed—or indeed only one. Mary has chosen what is better, and it will not be taken away from her."

Luke 10:41-42

I can use the house to create a home. I can offer my family, my friends, myself, and even strangers the gift of love by making them feel special when they are in my home.

Sarah Mae

My husband and I sometimes watch *Tidying Up with Marie Kondo* on Netflix. In this series of inspiring home makeovers, Marie works with families whose homes are disorganized, cluttered, and chaotic. The families living inside seemed stressed and most definitely overwhelmed. Over the course of a month or so, Marie comes in and helps them transform their homes into spaces that are enjoyable, organized, and restful! When she makes her final visit into the home, the families welcome her with open arms, smiling faces, and usually some grateful tears. They are overcome by the peace she has brought to their homes and can't seem to find the words to thank her enough.

In one episode, a mother who was trying to organize a heap of laundry asked Marie, desperately, "Do you have kids? How do you get them to clean up?" Marie responded, "They just see me do it and I enjoy myself and I make it fun to clean together." I think Marie is on to something!

I do not know about you, but often, my own go-to homemaking attempts are just me barking at my children to clean their rooms, huffing and puffing as I try to get "all the things" done. In those moments, homemaking is not fun at all; it's stressful. I want my home to feel as if you've been wrapped in a warm hug when you enter it—a place where my family can rest, a place where they can retreat, and a place where they can fill their love tanks.

It is a little tradition around here that before my husband comes home, the kids and I always take about twenty or thirty minutes to clean up the house. My husband appreciates a clean home after a long day at work. I have had many, many times when these twenty to thirty minutes have literally been the most stressful part of the day for all of us. Mostly because I choose to let the task take over the heart of what is trying to be accomplished. When I bark orders at my kids and act completely overwhelmed, the whole house can feel my frustration, and it usually doesn't end well. The result is that we will have a clean house but at the expense of everyone walking on eggshells around Mom.

On the contrary, when I have taken time to explain to my children that it shows Dad how much we love him when we create a peaceful home for him to come home to, they all get a little pep in their step to do an extra great job. Just the other day, my oldest, who is nine, said to me, "Mom, I know you have been overwhelmed at how messy the house has been today, but when it was time to clean, you seemed happy! It makes me feel like today is a good day!" The heart behind how we make our homes matters. Our kids are watching us, and we set the tone for the mood in our homes more than we know.

I adore the story of Mary and Martha in the Bible on this very topic (Luke 10:38-42). It is simple but profound. Martha opened her home to Jesus as He was traveling. Her sister Mary was also at the home. The story goes on to say that Martha was busy, trying to prepare and being somewhat of a busybody. However, Mary just sat at the feet of Jesus and listened to Him. Jesus remarked that Mary had "chosen what is better." I wonder if we too could take this same, gentle challenge in our homes, choosing what is better over our rigid task list! We could snuggle up with our kids and read more, taking the time to smile and tell them how much we adore them. We could listen to our children talk about video games for the billionth time with enthusiasm rather than multitasking to keep getting chores done. We could plan a small in-home date night with our husbands after the kids go to bed, popping popcorn and cozying up next to each other on the couch rather than loading the dishwasher.

I believe that Jesus is in the "tidying up" business as well. While He may not be broadcasted on a popular media platform like Netflix, He makes His mark in the hidden places of our hearts. He whispers to us "tidying tips" of love, grace, forgiveness, and sweet traditions to implement with our families at home. He gives us a vision of the kind of home that our hearts long for and the kind of home our family will treasure for years to come.

Jesus is not concerned with the state of our laundry basket or if our drawers are organized. He cares about our hearts and how we love those in our homes. He cares about that "warm hug" and about a gentle smile as we go through our mundane days. We can rest assured that the laundry will keep piling day after day and that dishes will return to the sink, but through it all, we can take heart that we "chose what was better."

FAITH-FILLED IDEA:
Have Fun by Setting a Timer

Setting a timer is an amazing motivator for staying focused on a chore (for you or the kids)! If you have kitchen, laundry, or any household chore to accomplish and you need a jump start as your energy starts to fade, try setting a timer. This method encourages you to beat the time you have set, stay hyperfocused on that one desired chore, and find out that it usually takes less time than you think to complete it. If you beat your time, have a little treat or reward ready.

36

Finding Beauty in Imperfection

········· TARA DAVIS ·········

*By wisdom a house is built, and through
understanding it is established; through knowledge
its rooms are filled with rare and beautiful treasures.*

Proverbs 24:3-4

*Redemption is not perfection. The redeemed
must realize their imperfections.*

John Piper

Some days I look around my house and all I notice are the kid messes, the crumbs, the worn-out furniture made soft from years of little-boy blanket forts, the muddy footprints by the door, and the outdated fixtures gracing nearly every corner of our home. When my eyes are focused on the critical, I am only able to see ugliness and chaos swirling around me. I grow discouraged and feel like a failure. I think of the other moms—the "better" moms—with Pinterest houses and presumably perfect lives, and my heart yearns for beauty (and maybe even just an ounce of perfection every now and then).

My friend, do you long to make your home a beautiful place for your family? I think we all do. God formed us with an innate desire to fill the world around us with beauty in some way (Ephesians 2:10). And often more than anything, we have a heart for creating a safe haven for our family, a refuge from the storms of life in which they feel comfortable, loved, and cherished.

However, when our search for beauty becomes striving for perfection in our home, we lose sight of God's desires for us. Our quest for beauty morphs into a dissatisfaction that will tear down our home instead of build it up. But may I let you in on a little secret? It is not so much about the beautiful atmosphere you create; candles, food, and decor are wonderful, but it is a mother's soul, radiantly lit with the glow of the Holy Spirit, that fills a home with grace and eliminates the need for perfection (Romans 15:13).

Sister, when you are walking in the Spirit, your loving words and a gentleness, which can only come from Jesus, will fill the corners of your home and the hearts of your family. They will be drawn in by your kindness and joy, and they will be enthralled with the love of the Father as they see you walking with Him (Matthew 5:16).

However, to be able to walk in the Spirit of Christ, we must change our vision. We must choose to take off our glasses of criticism, comparison, and perfection and replace them with lenses that look to the things Jesus exemplifies: love, compassion, and grace. How can we put these qualities into action within the four walls of our home?

My friend, we can refocus our vision on the things that create a sense of joy and peace within our family. We can appreciate the little messes throughout our house—our husband's shoes laid awry, tiny fingerprints on the windows, Play-Doh bits and toast crumbs dusting the floor—as evidence of our most valued family members who live within. We can look at our aging floors and countertops as a stress-free blessing to little kids who like to play hard. We can ask our husbands and children to help with decorating, allowing them to make our home their own. We can celebrate the forts and worn-out furniture, as there will be a time down the road for more order and nicer things. But now is the perfect time to cherish the imperfect season in which you abide!

Let go of perfection, my friend! Christ shining through you is what truly makes your home beautiful. Be the mama who looks past the flaws and sees the heart of your family. Lean into the Lord, seeking Him diligently every day. Let Him refocus your vision to the things He values, allowing yourself to shine with the dazzling love of Jesus to the precious ones within your home!

FAITH-FILLED IDEA: Be Intentional

Proverbs 14:1 tells us that "the wise woman builds her house." Are you building lasting, eternal qualities into your home, or is your construction only as deep as the color of your walls and the décor on your mantle? We can light candles, turn on music, and pop homemade cookies into the oven, yet still have a home devoid of beauty—a home bankrupt of love, joy, and all the things God desires for our families. I would challenge you to be intentional about building into your "home" important qualities that will last for eternity. Check out the "Powerful Six List" on page 203 of the "HELPful Resources" to help you with this exercise!

37

The Art of Christian Hospitality

MARI JO MAST

Keep on loving each other as brothers and sisters. Don't forget to show hospitality to strangers, for some who have done this have entertained angels without realizing it.

Hebrews 13:1-2 NLT

The heart of hospitality is about creating space for someone to feel seen and heard and loved. It's about declaring your table a safe zone, a place of warmth and nourishment.

Shauna Niequest

I admit—I often cringe when I hear the word "hospitality." It feels like God continually challenges me in this area! I have a lot of flesh to conquer and misconceptions to let go of. I hate when I allow perfectionism to keep me from being hospitable.

Do you struggle too?

It seems hospitality is kind of rare these days. Which makes me question, What's the meaning of it in the truest sense, and what does it look like anyway?

Years ago, I remember my parents talking fondly of my dad's parents. They modeled hospitality in such a practical and simple way. Since they were missionaries for a large portion of their lives and pastors to a small Mennonite church, guests and friends arrived at their home (unannounced and at any time of day) to visit. Sometimes complete strangers (friends of friends) traveled out of state and needed a place to stay for the night. No matter who they were, my grandparents readily and graciously invited them inside and provided them with a snack or home-cooked meal, no matter how inconvenient! Often, they would offer a clean room, a warm bed, and an invitation to stay the night. Turning anyone away was simply out of the question. My grandparents loved hosting people in their home.

A very precious friend of mine also loves inviting people into her home and meeting their needs. She makes authentic and simple servanthood look easy. Her home, though very beautiful, never takes the spotlight. Guests feel appreciated when they enter, and the food she creates, though simple, is so nourishing and plenteous (I believe she prays over it—I have secretly wondered how it seems to multiply. Ha!). Those who eat at her table come away knowing it was a holy experience. The presence of God is tangibly felt. Leaving her home inspires me! I want my serving to be a form of worship around the table like hers, where heart-to-heart connections happen and fond memories are never forgotten.

Years ago, hospitality was a normal and a regular part of life, but let's be honest, times have changed. It's pretty common now to refer guests and friends alike to a hotel or restaurant nearby instead of welcoming them into our home (especially when we are unprepared). This makes me sad.

Hebrews 13:2 (NLT) has something interesting to say about allowing our homes to be accessible to anyone, even strangers. It gives us this reminder: "Don't forget to show hospitality to strangers, for some who have done this have entertained angels without realizing it!"

Hospitality must be really important to God for the Bible to say that! It sounds like it should be a normal part of our lives. This takes us to a whole new level of trust in God because today we are not encouraged to invite strangers into our homes. However, if the writer of Hebrews commanded it, we should keep our minds open to the idea. This makes me think, What if God's people all over the world would open their homes to strangers more often? What if we wouldn't worry so much about our lives or about being inconvenienced? I'm sure it would radically shift our culture! Imagine how many new friendships could be fostered and developed.

Have we sadly allowed extravagance, selfish materialism, and a perfectionist mindset to crowd out true hospitality? Has it kept us from simply loving and serving others (including angelic beings)? As believers, can we choose to live an authentic, humble life and let people who enter our homes see our warts and imperfections instead?

I'm honestly searching my own heart and asking God to change my thinking. Instead of being intimidated, I'm trying to choose humility. It's a breath of fresh air when I see things are not perfect (dirty dishes in the sink, mounds of laundry, little handprints on the windows) when I enter someone else's home. It makes me feel more relaxed and comfortable. I believe when I allow others to see my "mess" too, it gives them the freedom to do the same. If my home doesn't resemble *House Beautiful*, it doesn't matter. It's not about my house anyway, but rather, about keeping an open and warm heart to friendships being maintained, cultivated, and cherished whether old or new!

FAITH-FILLED IDEA: Host a Tea Party

Host a tea party and make scones as your featured snack. Invite your guests two weeks ahead of time and gather a cute table cloth, teapot, and teacups along with varieties of tea. Make the scones (recipe in "HELPful Resources" on page 211) a few hours before your party so they're nice and fresh! Try to initiate a heart-to-heart conversation and a beautiful time of sharing as you facilitate hospitality in your home.

38

Everyday Celebrations

RAE-ELLEN SANDERS

*They celebrate your abundant goodness
and joyfully sing of your righteousness.*

Psalm 145:7

*When God does it, we do more than
remember it—we celebrate it.*

Woodrow Kroll

I love to plan parties! I love to celebrate the people in my life with the things they love and that make them happy. Colored napkins, balloons, and root beer floats can change any regular day into one to remember. Party planning is just one way for me to love on others and make them feel special.

Did you know that God's Word points to many celebrations? Starting in the Old Testament, the Israelites commemorated the feasts unto the Lord as reminders of His faithfulness. They celebrated the harvest of their crops, wedding ceremonies, and victories from battle, all with great merriment. The Bible also emphasizes the jubilation of the prodigal's homecoming and the much-anticipated wedding feast of our returning King. Let's face it, our God likes to party and for us to celebrate with Him.

Our hearts as Christians should be so full of joy that we rejoice in the good days and even the bad ones. Philippians 4:4 says, "Rejoice in the Lord always. I will say it again: Rejoice!" Finding joy in even the smallest things lends reason to offering praise to our Creator. When we take time in our hurried lives to observe the little things, we are in essence living a life of gratitude. I have found that when I am grateful, my heart is happy. Counting blessings ultimately lifts my burdens and fills me with joy. Think of the message that you are conveying to your children when you recognize the little victories in your child's life.

Dear mama, don't be daunted: Turning something ordinary into something special can be a very delightful challenge! Minimal effort goes a long way to brightening every day. Money isn't even necessary to cherish someone or to recognize their smallest successes. Little touches make a difference!

- Throw a special tablecloth on your table, pick some wildflowers or pick a single bloom to decorate your table.
- Write a love note for your child or husband and place it in their lunch box, backpack, or briefcase.
- Using a dry erase marker, leave a note or Scripture on the bathroom mirror.
- Burn a candle or oils to make your home smell lovely and homey.
- Bake cookies or cook a special dinner and eat around the table together.
- Turn off the television and the cell phones to engage in uninterrupted conversation.
- Eat breakfast for dinner or have double desserts one night.
- Start traditions of "special plates" for the honoree, a dignified seating preference, or a grand breakfast in bed.
- Buy a joke book, laugh out loud, and make room for laughter.

Look for silliness in your circumstances and take time out of your busy schedules to try something different. Be an observer of how to celebrate the whole year round! If hospitality is not your gift like it is mine, ask the Lord for how-to steps in practicality or simply try to tweak whatever you already do. Think back to your own childhood memories. What do you remember fondly? Implement the things from your past that brought you joy.

My mom used to bake my twin brother's and my birthday cakes from scratch. She used to use all the fancy pastry bags and special tips to decorate the cake to look like our favorite characters. Birthdays were special affairs that I now try to re-create. Why not try re-creating a positive memory and make it special for your own children? The smell of bacon and eggs on a lazy Saturday morning or donut runs in our pajamas, an impromptu game night with popcorn and soda, campouts in the backyard staring at the stars and eating S'mores, Shirley Temples with extra cherries, banana splits or ice cream sundaes…these are all memories I cherish and want to relive with my family.

Get your kids involved! Ask your children to help look for ways to applaud and appreciate others, and then strategically plan and apply them. Teaching your kids to treasure moments and others is a skill that isn't caught but taught. Start new traditions that will build a chain of memories that will reach into the future!

FAITH-FILLED IDEA:
Celebrate with a Waffle Bar

Why not start your everyday celebrations tonight with breakfast for dinner! What could be more fun than a waffle bar with loads of chocolate chips, whipped cream, and various toppings? Your kids will love your spontaneity and want to adopt this exception to the rule. Turn to page 212 for a yummy homemade waffle recipe.

39

A Peaceful Home

MARI JO MAST

Always be humble and gentle. Be patient with each other, making allowance for each other's faults because of love. Make every effort to keep yourselves united in the Spirit, binding yourselves together with peace.

Ephesians 4:2-3 NLT

If our children have the background of a godly, happy home and this unshakable faith that the Bible is indeed the Word of God, they will have a foundation that the forces of hell cannot shake.

Ruth Bell Graham

admit, as a young parent, I expected a lot of perfection from my kids. I regret it now because my lofty ideals kept me from loving my children the way God wanted me to love them. Do you know what I mean?

Depending on how we respond, strife can either escalate or slowly be diminished in our home. We can't eradicate discord altogether, but a godly response to it can potentially lead to an atmosphere of love and peace instead of more strife.

Even today, sometimes when I think my children need more rules, what they really need is for me to show them a better way. How I parent plays a big role in their response. My attitude and actions can either lead them to Jesus or away from Him, and my goal as a mom is for my children to know and experience God. Behavior and rules alone can never change my child's sinful heart. Only God can do that.

Romans 2:4 (NLT) says, "Don't you see how wonderfully kind, tolerant, and patient God is with you? Does this mean nothing to you? Can't you see that his kindness is intended to turn you from your sin?"

Mama, did you know God's kindness is intended to turn us to Him instead of sin? He wants us to have a relationship with Him so that sin will lose its power over us!

Growing up, I didn't have a very accurate picture of God. I didn't see Him as a very kind, tolerant, or patient God, but instead, I saw Him as mad, far away, and harsh—like He wanted to keep track of all the bad things I did so He could punish me. The verse above in Romans 2:4 says He is just the opposite. It wasn't until I was in my late twenties that I realized He is kind, tolerant, and patient.

We parent better when we know God is patient and kind. Both of these attributes lead to a more peaceful environment in our home.

Mama, don't sweat the small stuff! When we become overwhelmed and desperate, we tend to parent out of our flesh instead of the Holy Spirit. God is so willing to teach us how to do this if we're willing to be taught. I often ask myself, "What would Jesus do in this situation?" as I parent.

God's Word transforms our parenting as we navigate through tough seasons of strife with our children. The Word is like a map with many pleasant roads, it shows where to back up and turn around, which direction to go, and what to do when we're confused.

When I open my Bible, I ask for God to help me understand what I'm reading, even though at times I can't wrap my puny brain around His ways.

I hope my examples encourage you to seek God as a mom. Though motherhood seems daunting at times, remember how short this season is. My children are older now, and I've found it to be true—before you know what is happening, your little babies will be all grown up and your nest will be empty! Give yourself permission to enjoy your children while you still can. Live with no regrets. Don't beat yourself up when you make a mistake, and remember it's never too late to start over! Never. Above everything else, remember God's faithfulness covers even your worst failures!

Let peace reign in your home by letting go of any unrealistic expectations, and let God lead you in your parenting!

FAITH-FILLED IDEA: Pray Before You Say

This week, try to filter your thoughts before you do any talking. "Pray before you say." Hug and kiss your kids—tell them you love them—especially when they mess up.

Scriptures to Pray for Your Home

Pray that those within your home will choose to serve the Lord.

> "But as for me and my household, we will serve the LORD" (Joshua 24:15).

Pray that Jesus Christ will be the foundation of your home.

> "For no one can lay any foundation other than the one already laid, which is Jesus Christ" (1 Corinthians 3:11).

Pray that God will give you wisdom and fill your home with beautiful spiritual treasures.

> "By wisdom a house is built, and through understanding it is established; through knowledge its rooms are filled with rare and beautiful treasures" (Proverbs 24:3-4).

Pray that God will make your home a place of peace.

> "When you enter a house, first say, 'Peace to this house'" (Luke 10:5).

Pray that everyone within your home will go to the Lord and find rest.

> "Come to me, all you who are weary and burdened, and I will give you rest" (Matthew 11:28).

Pray that God will keep your home safe.

"You alone, LORD, make me dwell in safety" (Psalm 4:8).

Pray that your home will be a place of generous hospitality.

"Offer hospitality to one another without grumbling" (1 Peter 4:9).

Pray that God will strengthen and protect all those within your home from evil.

"But the Lord is faithful, and he will strengthen you and protect you from the evil one" (2 Thessalonians 3:3).

Pray that God will make your home a secure place of rest.

"My people will live in peaceful dwelling places, in secure homes, in undisturbed places of rest" (Isaiah 32:18).

Pray that the Lord will meet all the needs within your home and family in accordance with His will.

"And my God will meet all your needs according to the riches of his glory in Christ Jesus" (Philippians 4:19).

Part 5

The Wise Woman Fosters Friendships

I remember reading a long time ago that there are two things that will determine your future besides your faith in Jesus Christ: the books you read and the people you hang out with. I hate to admit it, but as a young mom, I was so desperate for friends that I spent time with women who yelled at their kids and gossiped about their husbands behind their backs. The sad thing is that because of these influences in my life, I started being grouchier with my husband and kids too. Thankfully, God spoke to my heart and said that I need to be intentional about the types of friends that I hang around with and that choosing my friends wisely was just as important as encouraging my children to do the same.

Sweet one, we are not supposed to do this life alone. Cultivating godly friendships takes time and effort, but it is some of the most important time you will ever spend. God wants you to have iron-sharpening-iron friendships in your life (Proverbs 27:17)—people who will make you a better wife and mom. If you don't have these types of friends, pray and ask God to bring them to you. He is the giver of all good gifts and is faithful to provide what we need when we need it.

love, Deb

40

Friendship to Last a Lifetime

·················· DEB WEAKLY and MELISSA LAIN ··················

*Having loved his own who were in the
world, he loved them to the end.*

John 13:1

*You have not chosen one another, but I
have chosen you for one another.*

C.S. Lewis, *The Four Loves*

remember the first time I ever had an argument with my friend Melissa. It was about thirty years ago, and we were standing at the front desk of the hair salon we worked at after closing time. I turned to walk back to my station when she stopped me to chat about my current boyfriend. The conversation went well until she asked me the deeply personal question: "Is he a Christian?" As soon as the words left her lips, I felt embarrassed because I had never even thought about his faith. Hot anger began to rise up in me, and I scowled and responded, "Why do I care if he is a Christian? I'm not even a Christian!"

Can you believe I said that? I was quite a different person before I came to know Jesus! It turns out she was so wise in saying that to me because about a month later he went out with another girl while we were still dating, and I was heartbroken. I came to work the day after the breakup with my tail between my legs. Melissa never said, "I told you so," and she never gave up on me either. She knew I was a broken person in need of a Savior.

She even invited me to a Christian concert. I gave my heart to Jesus that night, and He began making big changes in the way I lived.

I am so glad Melissa didn't call it quits when I snapped at her. She still pursued a friendship with me and was a bridesmaid at my wedding to my Christian husband two years later. We are close friends, but complete opposites in personality. I love that part of our friendship; she has been and always will be one of my "iron sharpening iron" friends. We still have little fusses from time to time, but I am a much better person because I have her in my life. The truth is, friends who know you and are brave enough to speak into your life help make you a better person and should be treasured. Since we love to give "help" in the Help Club for Moms, Melissa and I decided to team up together to help you stay friends with your dear ones for many, many years to come. Take it away, Melissa!

It's so interesting to think back on that conversation. Deb was defensive, feisty, and angry at my question, but I knew in my heart God wanted me to share my faith and conviction with my friend. I wanted Deb to know Jesus and the deep love that He has for us, so when we went to that concert, I was so happy to see her walking down the aisle to accept Jesus. Just thinking about what the Lord has done in Deb's life and my life brings me great joy; and I'm so happy we are lifelong friends.

Are you longing for a lasting friendship? Is there a Deb or Melissa in your life? We are out there, and if you look, you will find one of us. Most likely you already have someone who needs you and whom you need, but it takes work to stay friends. In any relationship, there are times when you want to walk away without ever looking back. It can seem easier to just find a new friend. As we grow older, we may feel regret from losing contact with wonderful women in our lives because we didn't realize their value. Friends do come in and out of our life, so how do we keep valuable friendships for a lifetime?

Deb and I compiled a list in hopes of helping you cultivate great friendships:

- *If you don't have a friend, pray and ask God for one.* He is faithful to provide when we ask (Matthew 7:7).

- *Pray for yourself and your friends.* Ask God to help you be the best friend you can in the power of the Holy Spirit (Ephesians 6:18).

- *Love unconditionally.* Accept your friend's shortcomings and limitations. Don't expect her to be like you (1 Peter 4:8).

- *Be a reliable friend—it builds trust and respect.* Do what you say you're going to do, and let her know well in advance of any change in plans (Matthew 5:37).

- *Speak highly of her husband.* If you don't like him, find something nice to think and say about him. No one is perfect (Titus 2:4).

- *Encourage each other's kids.* Be the one who loves your friend's kids well, throughout every season of their lives. Her kids will never forget you (1 Thessalonians 5:11).

- *Don't impose your parenting ideals on your friends.* Let them walk with God, and trust them to parent the way God tells them (1 Thessalonians 4:11).

- *Remember, Satan hates your friendships. He will do what he can to bring division between yours.* Try to assume the best as much as possible (John 10:10; 1 Peter 5:8).

- *If you are upset with your friend, don't gossip to other people.* This only makes things worse. In fact, *never* gossip. Gossip destroys friendships (Proverbs 11:13; 20:19).

- *Make haste to settle conflict.* Don't let the devil get a foothold in your relationship. Pray and ask God to help you love her like Jesus and then humbly talk about the offense (Ephesians 4:31-32).

FAITH-FILLED IDEA: Share the Love

Take time to call, text, or write a handwritten note to your friends this week and share how they bless your life.

41

Forgiveness and Friendship

· RACHEL JONES ·

*Be kind and compassionate to one another, forgiving
each other, just as in Christ God forgave you.*

Ephesians 4:32

*Forgiveness is not an occasional
act; it is a constant attitude.*

Martin Luther King Jr.

Years ago, I was incapable of forgiveness. I was incredibly disappointed with someone I loved, and honestly, I just tried to pretend like it didn't happen. This person had acted without even considering my feelings, and I was mad! And to make matters worse, the unforgiveness in my heart and my frustration with the whole situation started impacting how I was treating my husband, my children, and even other friends who were not involved. I became short-tempered and was bothered more than I should have been.

I thought that if maybe enough time and space were present, the hurt would disappear and I could move on with my life. But Jesus wouldn't let me ignore or escape from what I was doing. You see, dear mama, Jesus won't stand for His daughters holding unforgiveness and bitterness in their hearts. I knew my relationship with this person needed to be mended. She was very important to me, and despite all this time, I loved her deeply. I began to search the Scriptures for God's truths and commands on love and forgiveness. I knew this journey would only happen if I trusted the Lord and allowed Him to transform and soften my heart.

To be completely honest, I felt disgraceful knowing that I was withholding forgiveness when Christ had first forgiven me. As Christians, the power—and the beauty—of our transformed life is that "it is God who works in you, both to will and to work for His good pleasure" (Philippians 2:13 ESV). Our humanness and sinfulness are not capable of forgiving heartless acts and attitudes. It is Christ's love and example transplanted into our believing hearts that can exchange our weakness for His strength. Through prayer, prayer, and even more prayer, I found the courage to submit my hurt and bitterness to the Lord and have *forgiven* the person who caused me pain. Now, I don't want you to think that I just prayed for a few days and *bam!* God intervened. This was a two-year process for me. The journey to a new and healthy relationship was not easy, but it was so worth it.

Over those years, I learned that we all have two choices when we get offended or hurt: We can pull away from love and the promise of a restored relationship, or we can choose to press into it. What does "pressing into love" mean? Jesus gives us an answer in Matthew 18:21-22 (ESV): "Then Peter came up and said to him, 'Lord, how often will my brother sin against me, and I forgive him? As many as seven times?' Jesus said to him, 'I do not say to you seven times, but seventy-seven times.'" So what is the point? As a Christ follower, we should never reach a place of unforgiveness; after all, we have that same love inside of us because we have the Holy Spirit!

The amazing thing about Jesus is that He didn't just tell us to forgive others, He showed us with His actions. Two great examples of forgiveness in Scripture are the beautiful story of Jesus's unconditional love and forgiveness toward the adulterous woman in John 8 and Christ's final words on the cross: "Father, forgive them; for they do not know what they are doing" (Luke 23:34). Wow! Jesus sure sets a high standard. But this is the standard that we should all be striving for. Mama, the effect from withholding forgiveness is huge, and this is seen so clearly within friendships. So much of the anger and strife that exists in relationships today is rooted in people's unwillingness to forgive.

I would like to challenge all of you today with one word—love. Proverbs 17:9 (NLT) states that "love prospers when a fault is forgiven." I personally think that what stops many people from granting forgiveness is that they believe if they forgive the person, they are condoning the "offender's" sin. Holding grudges only chains you to the past and causes bitterness, like a steady drip of toxin into your life. When forgiveness is given, I guarantee you a weight will be lifted off of you, and you will feel free and complete. Submit these broken friendships to your Father! There is no behavior that cannot be forgiven. After all, where would *we* be without the kindness, love, and forgiveness of Jesus?

FAITH-FILLED IDEA: Write a Letter

Write a sincere note to the person (or people) you need to forgive. Whether there is only one person or ten people total, spend time in prayer for them as you are writing. Submit your hurt and bitterness to Jesus. Pray over the letter for a week, and I guarantee you that you will feel softer toward them. Forgiveness is a process. Don't expect to be ready in two days. However, admitting you have unforgiveness is the first step. I am praying for you on this journey! If you feel strong enough, mail your letter.

42

On Loving Your Friends Well

RAE-ELLEN SANDERS

Oil and perfume make the heart glad;
so does the sweetness of a friend's
counsel that comes from the heart.

Proverbs 27:9 AMP

By friendship you mean the greatest love, the
greatest usefulness, the most open communication,
the noblest sufferings, the severest truth, the
heartiest counsel, and the greatest union of minds
of which brave men and women are capable.

Jeremy Taylor

A true friendship is such a gift! If you have the fortune of having a true friend, you know that friendship is not always easy, but the effort is always worth it. Friendship like any relationship needs to be nurtured and safe guarded. Mama, God intended for us to have friends and for us to pour into one another! He wants us to hold each other's hands up in trying times and to share a word of encouragement in season. Maybe you have allowed some of your friendships to fizzle out because of busyness, or perhaps there is unforgiveness for something that was harshly said, or perhaps a misunderstanding hasn't been rectified between you. Christian friendship needs to point to *grace*!

Let me encourage you go to your friend and ask to start fresh. It's quite biblical to go to your neighbor and confess wrongdoing. Matthew 5:23-24 (NKJV) states, "Therefore if you bring your gift to the altar, and there remember that your brother has something against you, leave your gift there before the altar, and go your way. First be reconciled to your brother, and then come and offer your gift." God loves to restore relationships. Will you pray about whom you need to reconnect with and possibly apologize to? Commit to pray for these friends and with your friends! Set aside time and make an effort to connect on a personal level.

How many of us have grown up hearing our parents quote the Golden Rule multiple times a day? "Do unto others as you would have them do unto you." I have followed my mama's habit out of necessity, with five kids at home to teach and correct on how to love one another. I can be heard touting the same verbiage daily. I desire for my children to be kind and to treat others with respect. I want to teach them that in order to have friends, you have to be a friend. A *tangible* one! In Colossians 3, we are exhorted to actively pursue being a godly friend to others, to actively pursue patience, forgiveness, love, and thanksgiving. By pursuing others this way, we extend a friendship that we desire.

I love the exercise of loving others in their love language. This is very rewarding in marriage but can also be applied to friendships! We should love our friends in the language that ministers to their hearts. If your friend loves gifts, then bring a cup of coffee or tea next time you see her. If she appreciates acts of service, offer to watch her kiddos so she can run errands or help her fold laundry while visiting. If she loves words of affirmation, jot down a note telling her how much you appreciate her. If your friend appreciates physical touch, make sure to hug her hello and goodbye. If quality time is her love language, make sure to carve out enough time to go shopping or just sit and chat. If you don't know what makes your friend's heart feel full, simply ask her or try all the above suggestions! Watch to see which one blesses her the most, and then treasure your friend as the gift she is!

FAITH-FILLED IDEA: Ways to Go Deeper

Are you the type of friend others want to be around or can count on? God can help us be sensitive to the needs of our friends. Ask the Lord about going deeper with your friendships, including loving your friends' children, praying for your friends' marriages, and forgiving a friend's hurtful offense. Ask the Lord to help you lend a listening ear more often or manage your time better so you can just sit and be there. Perhaps you need to extend love to a friend through an act of kindness—going the extra mile by making a meal or lending a hand with child-care or perhaps by just offering a shoulder to cry on, a hug, or a smile when celebrating a small success. There are so many different ways to show tangible love and embrace our friendships!

Most of us love the way we want to be loved. So I find myself doing kind things to bless others, otherwise known as acts of service. It fills my boat to love in this way. Last year for my friend Rachel's birthday, I made her favorite dessert—carrot cake with cream cheese frosting. It was a labor of love but worth the effort. If you want authentically amazing carrot cake, try my recipe on page 214 in the "HELPful Resources."

43

Seasons of Loneliness— Praying for Friends

·········· TARA DAVIS ··········

*The LORD is good to those whose hope is in
him, to the one who seeks him; it is good to
wait quietly for the salvation of the LORD.*

Lamentations 3:25-26

*Loneliness, like every form of suffering, is passing
away for those who love him. Ahead of you is
the full family fellowship of God and all of his
redeemed saints forever. The day is nearing when
you will know him as you have been fully known.*

John Piper

Can I let you in on a little secret about me? I'm *that* girl—you know, the one who has always been a little different, who says things that elicit an awkward silence, who sits at the lunch table by herself. Much of that was in my youth, of course, but in my mind, I am still that girl. Let's just gloss over years of socially awkward memories by saying that making friends has never been easy for me. There have been some long years of loneliness for my little old heart, but oh, how God has used those lonely years to do some extra special work in my heart! And decades later, I have seen Him abundantly answer my prayers for friends!

Girl, how is *your* heart? Is it overflowing with quiet loneliness?

165

Sometimes it seems that the quest for adult friendships is as difficult as it was when we were younger. I always felt it would get easier, that the days of rejection and walking through life in solitude would be long gone. That isn't always the case. Good friends are often hard to find. God loves every part of you though! His adoration for you is as infinite as time itself. He holds your lonely heart in His gentle hands and provides supernatural healing.

The Lord desires that we trust Him with our friendships. Pray that He will bring friends into your life to sharpen you and encourage you in your walk with Him (Proverbs 27:17). God's plan for you is to walk through life in fellowship with others, and He will meet your need for friendship in His timing. Perhaps, like me, the Lord will bring you a close circle of godly friends after many, many years of prayer.

While you are waiting for Him to bring close relationships in your life, draw near to Him (James 4:8). Look for the ways He wishes to refine you. He wants to change you to be more like Him. Sometimes loneliness is the catalyst to that change, the means of becoming more compassionate, humble, and loving. Allow Him work in your heart as only He is able.

If you have been striving for connection in this world, Jesus wants you to rest in Him for a while (Matthew 11:28-30). Give Him your burdens; He can carry them better than any person (1 Peter 5:7). Talk to Him; He is never too busy or preoccupied. Listen for Him. His whispers of love are nearly constant; we simply need to quiet our spirit to hear them.

Perhaps you have friends who love you and whom you love in return, but you still feel the ache of emptiness and isolation. That is normal, my sweet sister! We are not made to be completely filled by another person. Our husbands, children, parents, and friends are unable to entirely fill the void within us. We have an intense need for our Father. He is the only one who can pervade the lonely chasms in our heart and make us whole and complete. With Him, we can be filled with so much love it overflows to those around us. He is our most perfect friend!

You are precious to the Lord (Isaiah 43:4). He will lift your head, dry your tears, and fill the loneliness in your heart with His love and grace. He will provide His own companionship to meet the needs of your heart in ways you cannot begin to imagine (Philippians 4:19). Will you trust Him with your heart today, my friend?

FAITH-FILLED IDEA: Encourage Someone Today

It is possible that you are the answer to someone else's longtime prayer for a friend. Find someone to encourage today! Perhaps you know a woman who seems lonely—write her an encouraging note to let her know you are praying for her. Finally, during this time of waiting for friends, allow the Lord to mold you into the type of friend you would like to have. His gentle hands can help you become more patient, kind, and trustworthy if you allow Him to do His beautiful work in your heart!

44

The Power of Praying Together

· MARI JO MAST ·

*I am praying not only for these disciples but
also for all who will ever believe in me through
their message. I pray that they will all be one,
just as you and I are one—as you are in me,
Father, and I am in you. And may they be in us
so that the world will believe you sent me.*

John 17:20-21 NLT

*Our prayers may be awkward. Our attempts
may be feeble. But since the power of prayer is
in the one who hears it and not in the one who
says it, our prayers do make a difference.*

Max Lucado

Praying with a friend used to intimidate me—I didn't want to expose my heart in my ramblings. What if she thought I sounded silly and was too emotional if I cried? What if it felt awkward and we didn't connect? Being a more private person, I wasn't convinced it was worth it to open up, to become vulnerable about some things in my life.

Let me tell you how this all changed.

I am an ordinary fortysomething mom married to an extraordinarily patient, loving guy (I really mean that). Our seven kiddos (three are married now) are completely normal—rambunctious, crazy, adorable, stiff-necked, rebellious, beautiful, stubborn, sweet, and heartwarming. Ha! Make sense?

When I was in the thick of raising my seven children a few years ago, a good friend approached me with this idea—what if we committed to pray for each other, our families, our husbands, and those around us, once a week? We were both smack dab in the middle of raising our larger than average families, groping for life as moms. We desperately wanted to come out on the other end at least halfway sane with our families intact. Above all, we wanted our kids to pursue truth and to love God with all their hearts.

Oh, friend, it happened at just the right time—suddenly it made sense. I didn't just want to pray with a friend; I *needed* it. So I agreed, and our partnership in prayer began.

I didn't know at the time how God would use these prayers to drastically change our lives. They made a tangible difference in our families and soon became our lifeline. We prayed bold faith-filled prayers and were one big praying mess as we wept, vulnerably shared our failures, and willingly became transparent with one another. We spoke out the truth of God's Word and witnessed miracles along the way. My friend and I grew closer in unity until we became inseparable. We were holy mamas, crying out for Jesus and asking what He wanted in our lives.

I can honestly say, while it's great to talk with a friend or do lots of fun things, it's absolutely priceless to *pray* with her—especially if she's a godly woman who cares enough to know and understand what is going on in your life (the good, the bad, and the ugly). Someone who steadfastly prays faith-filled prayers from the Word, helps lift you up, and stands with you to believe for God's best until you experience the answer to your prayers.

Girl, praying with a friend changed my life in so many ways!

I find strength and power as I pray with other women now. I'm not ashamed anymore because I know God hears our every word. Prayer meets a deep need inside our hearts—the need to be in unity with the Spirit of God and with each other. Unity is what Jesus was praying for in John 17:20-26 when He prayed that we would all be one. Jesus is with us when we pray.

Years later, I still pray with other moms. For the past few years, God has added the Help Club for Moms to my life, providing an even larger circle of beautiful prayer partners committed to doing life together. We try to do a ten-minute prayer call once a week and, oh, my goodness, the difference that little phone call can make!

Miracles have come out of this! Of course, praying together takes commitment, but I don't know where I would be today without the prayers of my friends. I can't afford *not* to commit!

There are lots of lonely moms looking for someone to pray with, and you might be one of them. Simply ask God to connect you with someone and then watch who He brings across your path. All you need is another godly, transparent, and willing person, and honestly, they are not hard to find. Simply be friendly, and ask if they would like to pray and do real life with you. I know how scary it is to be vulnerable in prayer, but the return is so worth it! I guarantee your life will never be the same.

As time progresses and culture keeps changing, it's more important than ever to be devoted to each other in prayer. Our prayers shift the atmosphere around us and give God permission to work miracles in our lives.

Dear one, I'm praying the Holy Spirit brings you a faith-filled friend to bust wide open the gates of heaven as you pray together. God desires it—I know He will bring her to you. Pray and watch for her today!

FAITH-FILLED IDEA: Make a Prayer Call

Now it's time to put feet to your faith and try something new! Pray and say, "God please bring a praying friend to me." Watch and see who God brings to you. Step out in faith and ask her to pray once a week for ten minutes. If she's hesitant, tell her to try to commit only for a month. When it's time to pray, stick to your time limit and simply say, "I'm calling for our ten-minute prayer call. How can I pray for you?" After each of you shares your needs, take a moment to pray together for those requests. If you would like to chat longer, plan to do so at another time (other than the prayer call). That way she doesn't think the calls to pray will take too long.

45

On Comparing Ourselves to Others

KRYSTLE PORTER

Each of you must examine your own actions. Then you can be proud of your own accomplishments without comparing yourself to others.

Galatians 6:4 GW

How much time he gains who does not look to see what his neighbor says or does or thinks, but only at what he does himself, to make it just and holy.

Marcus Aurelius

Comparison steals our joy, my friend. Surely, it doesn't take a rocket scientist to figure that out. It takes just a few minutes of being with other moms or friends to start the comparison game. Immediately our minds go to "Wow, she keeps her house really clean. I should keep a cleaner house." "She looks great and has lost some weight. I should probably join a gym and start to work out." "Look, she is going on another date with her husband. My husband hasn't asked me to go on a date in a long time. My husband must not love me as much as hers does." "She seems like she has so much patience with her kids. I lose my temper so fast. Why can't I be more like that?" "Her kids are so well behaved. Why do my kids embarrass me so much? I should go on online and order some books on this so I can get my kids on the right track."

Have you ever found yourself having thoughts like this? You are not alone if you have. So many of us struggle with comparison. The lies that we start believing about ourselves because we compare ourselves with others hurt us and hurt those around us. We find ourselves not being able to live in the capacity God gave each of us because we fear that we are less than, which could not be further from the truth!

The opposite of comparison is contentment. Let your heart meditate on these verses for a moment:

- "Godliness with contentment is great gain, for we brought nothing into the world, and we cannot take anything out of the world. But if we have food and clothing, with these we will be content" (1 Timothy 6:6-8 ESV).

- "Take care, and be on your guard against all covetousness, for one's life does not consist in the abundance of his possessions" (Luke 12:15 ESV).

We are not able to pull back the curtain on someone else's life to see their hidden spaces and struggles. All we can see is what is displayed for us through social media or what people are willing to share with us—which oftentimes is just a small glimpse of who they are or what their day was really like!

If you were able to look at people as Jesus does, comparison would not exist because we would look at others with eyes of love. We would appreciate everyone's different gifts and talents and respect their individuality. God created us to stand in uniqueness for a reason. Someone out there needs your specific personality to minister to them. You are just one piece in God's intricate puzzle of beauty in this big world. Without you being you, His puzzle would not be complete. Jesus doesn't need a replica piece. He needs you to be who He created you to be!

To be a great friend and one who can love another well, we need to be able to look at our dear friends as Jesus would, appreciating their gifts and struggles, accepting the life circumstances that make them who they are, and looking on them without envy because we can take nothing out of this world—not our good looks, money, possessions, home decorations, or perfectly organized dressers. All we take with us is the character and soul of who God made us to be. As we adjust our focus and start to view our friends in these ways, God will transform our hearts. We will start to appreciate our friends' talents and lean on their strengths. Comparisons will start to slip away. In return, we will be able to confidently offer our own strengths to others, knowing that we have something of worth to offer.

Sister, let us not allow comparison to steal our joy! Instead, let us allow contentment to rule our hearts, finding joy in our own family, our own provisions that God has given us, and the people God made us to be.

FAITH-FILLED IDEA:
Write a Few Thank-You Notes

Write a couple of thank-you notes to some dear friends this week. Tell them that you are thankful for their friendship, and be sure to add some specific things that you love about them. There is nothing like feeling loved and appreciated!

Then write out a note to God. Thank Him for who He made you to be. Ask Him to keep revealing little ways He made you uniquely you. Take time to genuinely write down your own character traits and strengths. Remember, God loves you deeply and knit you together in your mother's womb (Psalm 139:13). Not a single bit of who you are was made by accident but with the utmost thought and care.

46

How Friends Have Impacted My Life

·············· DEB WEAKLY ··············

Likewise, teach the older women to be reverent in the way they live, not to be slanderers or addicted to much wine, but to teach what is good. Then they can urge the younger women to love their husbands and children, to be self-controlled and pure, to be busy at home, to be kind, and to be subject to their husbands, so that no one will malign the word of God.

Titus 2:3-5

We make a living by what we get; we make a life by what we give.

Winston Churchill

When my children were young and still in our home, my husband and our daughter loved the Narnia series by C.S. Lewis. I remember the two of them sitting on her bed one evening after they read the last page of the final book, *The Last Battle*. There was a sense of accomplishment as they finished all seven books in the series but also a sense of sadness as it was all over. That's exactly how I felt after our kids grew up and left home. There was such a sense of accomplishment at what God had done in our family—Christie and Jack love Jesus with their whole hearts and are our best friends, but there was still an emptiness.

During this new season, I began to feel a spirit of depression coming over me. In my devotional time, I began pouring out my heart to God and asking Him to help me know what to do during this new phase in my life. I came across a passage in Scripture I had read many times before, but now it seemed to jump off the page: Titus 2:3-5, our key verse for this article, became such an anthem verse to me. I began to see my calling right there in black and white: to help the next generation learn how to create a godly home. I thought about all the godly women who had taught me during motherhood and how I wanted to now do the same, and finally, I remembered these sheets of paper I had kept in a box for twenty-one years called, "The H.E.L.P. Club."

Many years ago, I worked in Mary Kay Cosmetics to earn some money on the side. During that time, my director, Shirley, sat me down to help me learn how to run my business. She was an amazing, godly older woman who was also an army chaplain's wife. She showed me this document called "The Weekly Plan Sheet" and said, "Deb, first things first. If you're going to be successful in your Mary Kay business, you first have to spend time with God. So write down on this weekly plan sheet when you're going to read your Bible and pray." This is where my habit of reading my Bible began, which changed my life forever!

Shirley then told me about an opportunity to work with her senior director, Martie, another amazing older, godly woman. She was leading a twenty-four-week program called the "H.E.L.P Club"—which stood for "Headed for Leadership Position." Martie hand-typed every page of a twenty-four-week course that included a short and simple Bible study, something to focus on for your Mary Kay business, and something to do in your home with your kids each day. These simple sheets, delivered in the mail each week, transformed my life. They must have held a very special place in my heart because I kept them with me for more than twenty years through various moves and could never quite get rid of them!

I felt a strong desire in my heart to write a book for moms, using the H.E.L.P. Club sheets as a model for the manuscript. I received some great feedback from an author friend of mine to start a test pilot group to help process the idea and the content with me. The women in this group all helped to shape what is now the Help Club for Moms. Within this group were a few close friends of mine, who were devoted women deeply desiring to help other moms. I asked them to go a step further and come alongside me to form an all-volunteer ministry committed to the mission of "moms encouraging moms to know the love of Christ." As a team, we began writing practical Bible studies designed to help moms know Jesus more intimately and to create Christ-centered atmospheres in their homes. Eventually, we began establishing the Help Club for Moms in churches across the nation. It was thrilling to us because we love encouraging moms just like you!

Nine of these powerful women you have already met while reading this book: Mari Jo, Brandi, Tara, Rachel, Krystle, Rae-Ellen, Jennifer, Kristall, and Melissa. I wish I had known these ladies when my kids were growing up; they have truly impacted my life, as I pray they have impacted yours too. We all live imperfect lives with real families, but one thing is for sure, we all depend on Jesus and are committed to our friendships no matter what! I pray you feel a connection with one or all of them, almost like you have kindred spirits right here in this book. Be sure to read their bios in the back of the book on page 219 to get a feel for the lives we live with our families.

FAITH-FILLED IDEA:
Pray for Three Powerful Friends

As a young mom, I remember reading "He who walks with the wise will become wise" (Proverbs 13:20 BSB) and feeling so convicted about the friends I was hanging around with. I heard it said that we should always have three key friendships in our life: someone who is older and ahead of you in life, someone who is in the same stage of life as you, and someone younger who you can pour into. I encourage you to find these three women in your own life. Your life will be deeply impacted by these godly friendships, and so will your children. Walking with wise friends will change your life!

Scriptures to Pray for Friendships

Pray that God will be glorified in your friendships.

> "Not to us, LORD, not to us but to your name be the glory, because of your love and faithfulness" (Psalm 115:1).

Pray that there will be peace in your friendships.

> "If it is possible, as far as it depends on you, live at peace with everyone" (Romans 12:18).

Pray that you will be a loving friend at all times, even in times of adversity.

> "A friend loves at all times, and a brother is born for a time of adversity" (Proverbs 17:17).

Pray that you will faithfully use your gifts to serve your friends.

> "Each of you should use whatever gift you have received to serve others, as faithful stewards of God's grace in its various forms" (1 Peter 4:10).

Pray that as a friend, you will demonstrate the fruits of the Spirit.

> "But the fruit of the Spirit is love, joy, peace, forbearance, kindness, goodness, faithfulness, gentleness and self-control. Against such things there is no law" (Galatians 5:22-23).

Pray that God will give you wisdom to offer heartfelt advice to a friend in time of need.

> "Perfume and incense bring joy to the heart, and the pleasantness of a friend springs from their heartfelt advice" (Proverbs 27:9).

Pray that God will bring you, your husband, and your children good friends and direct you away from bad company.

> "Do not be misled: 'Bad company corrupts good character'" (1 Corinthians 15:33).

Pray that you will find wise friends and be a wise friend.

> "Walk with the wise and become wise, for a companion of fools suffers harm" (Proverbs 13:20).

Pray that you will be a forgiving friend, just as God has forgiven you.

> "Bear with each other and forgive one another if any of you has a grievance against someone. Forgive as the Lord forgave you" (Colossians 3:13).

Pray that the Lord will bless your friend, be gracious to her, and give her peace.

> "The Lord bless you and keep you; the Lord make his face shine on you and be gracious to you; the Lord turn his face toward you and give you peace" (Numbers 6:24-26).

Part 6

HELPful Resources

Here is your toolbox for practical ways to cultivate your spirit, love your husband, love your children, care for your home, and foster friendship.

Visit **myhelpclubformoms.com** and enter the code **thanks4moms** to access your free bonus content and printables.

47

The Wise Woman Cultivates Her Spirit

HOW TO MAKE A PRAYER BOARD
Rae-Ellen Sanders

Do you long for more time with the Lord but get caught up in the busyness of the day? Don't get me wrong; sometimes we don't have the luxury of long times of prayer. However, if we set aside time to have deliberate quiet time, we will be rejuvenated and rewarded with His presence. Ask the Lord to help you put aside what hinders you from seeking Him and to give you a passion for intercession. Building your prayer board takes a bit of intentionality.

First, acquire a trifold board, glue sticks, and scissors from an office store. Next, research verses and pictures that inspire you to pray. Print them or cut them out to glue on your board. Pinterest is a wonderful resource for finding graphic Scripture. Line up how you want your board to look and glue them on. Perhaps you'll like to write your favorite verses or Scriptures to remind you to pray against the enemy. When this is finished, it will be unique to you! Remember to take out your board and use it to shield/segregate yourself from the world to have time in uninterrupted prayer. This type of quiet time only scratches the surface of what God desires and commands us to do.

HOW TO MAKE A PRAYER BINDER
Deb Weakly

The first step in making your prayer binder is to start in prayer asking God for specific prayers for your family. If you are in the habit of journaling, write prayers the Lord shows you so you can put them in your binder.

The next step is to make sure you have each of the items on the supply list.

Be sure to take your time in preparing your prayer binder so that it reflects you. You can adapt the binder to suit your needs. As we often say in the Help Club for Moms, "You do you!" Below, I share how I break down my binder topics and a few of my prayers, but my heart's desire is for you to pray and ask God what He wants you to write in your binder.

Supplies

- small three-ring binder with a clear plastic front so you can slide a piece of paper behind the plastic and customize your prayer binder
- ten to twenty translucent sheet protectors
- notebook paper that will fit in the sheet protectors
- decorative paper if you want to be creative
- seven dividers with tabs

My binder is simply a three-ring binder with the clear plastic page protectors. I have organized my prayers into sections using the dividers with tabs. This way, I have only a few things to pray for each day.

My Dividers

- *Monday*: prayers for my husband and my marriage—fun, communication, intimacy, finances, and so on
- *Tuesday*: prayers for my children

- *Wednesday*: prayers for others—parents, in-laws, friends, people in our church, missionaries, and so on
- *Thursday*: prayers for myself to remember what is most important in this life and for God to help me be a good wife and mama
- *Friday*: prayers for our children's education
- *Saturday*: Scriptures that I love to pray and keep in front of me to remember
- *Sunday*: Sunday sermon notes and things the Lord is teaching me

For a complete list of the prayers in my binder, visit https://helpclubformoms.com/how-to-make-a-prayer-binder/.

REPLACING LIES WITH TRUTH
Kristall Willis

LIE: *I am a bad mom.*

TRUTH: "And we know that in all things God works for the good of those who love him, who have been called according to his purpose" (Romans 8:28).

"For we are God's handiwork, created in Christ Jesus to do good works, which God prepared in advance for us to do" (Ephesians 2:10).

LIE: *I am invisible.*

TRUTH: "If I go up to the heavens, you are there; if I make my bed in the depths, you are there" (Psalm 139:8).

"He will give you another Helper, that He may abide with you forever—the Spirit of truth...for He dwells with you and will be in you. I will not leave you orphans; I will come to you" (John 14:16-18 NKJV).

LIE: *I am not good enough, and I will not accomplish anything worthwhile.*

TRUTH: "I have raised you up for this very purpose, that I might show you my power and that my name might be proclaimed in all the earth" (Exodus 9:16).

"The LORD will fulfill his purpose for me; your steadfast love, O LORD, endures forever. Do not forsake the work of your hands" (Psalm 138:8 ESV).

"Many are the plans in a person's heart, but it is the LORD's purpose that prevails" (Proverbs 19:21).

"Whoever believes in me will do the works I have been doing, and they will do even greater things than these, because I am going to the Father. And I will do whatever you ask in my name, so that the Father may be glorified in the Son. You may ask me for anything in my name, and I will do it" (John 14:12-14).

"I am the vine; you are the branches. If you remain in me and I in you, you will bear much fruit; apart from me you can do nothing" (John 15:5).

LIE: *I am weak and useless.*

TRUTH: "He gives strength to the weary and increases the power of the weak" (Isaiah 40:29).

"Come to me, all you who are weary and burdened, and I will give you rest. Take my yoke upon you and learn from me, for I am gentle and humble in heart, and you will find rest for your souls. For my yoke is easy and my burden is light" (Matthew 11:28-30).

"I can do all things through Christ who strengthens me" (Philippians 4:13 NKJV).

LIE: *I can't let go of my past.*

TRUTH: "Forget the former things; do not dwell on the past. See, I am doing a new thing" (Isaiah 43:18-19).

"Therefore, if anyone is in Christ, the new creation has come: The old has gone, the new is here" (2 Corinthians 5:17).

"You were taught, with regard to your former way of life, to put off your old self, which is being corrupted by its deceitful desires; to be made new in the attitude of your minds; and to put on the new self, created to be like God in true righteousness and holiness" (Ephesians 4:22-24).

"Set your minds on things above, not on earthly things. For you died, and your life is now hidden with Christ in God...Put to death, therefore, whatever belongs to your earthly nature...and have put on the new self, which is being renewed in knowledge in the image of its Creator" (Colossians 3:2-17).

LIE: *I am fearful, anxious, and full of worry.*

TRUTH: "The LORD is with me; I will not be afraid. What can mere mortals do to me?" (Psalm 118:6).

"Therefore I tell you, do not worry about your life...Can any one of you by worrying add a single hour to your life?...Therefore do not worry about tomorrow, for tomorrow will worry about itself" (Matthew 6:25-34).

"Do not be anxious about anything, but in every situation, by prayer and petition, with thanksgiving, present your requests to God" (Philippians 4:6).

LIE: *I am not beautiful.*

TRUTH: "So God created mankind in his own image" (Genesis 1:27).

"I praise you because I am fearfully and wonderfully made; your works are wonderful, I know that full well" (Psalm 139:14).

"You are altogether beautiful, my darling; there is no flaw in you" (Song of Songs 4:7).

EASY CROCK-POT TACO SOUP
Rae-Ellen Sanders

Sometimes we just need to take advantage of modern technology in the kitchen—I am talking about the quintessential make-your-life-easy programmable Crock-Pot! This recipe yields a double portion for a large family of seven like mine.

Ingredients

2 lbs. ground beef, cooked in skillet

2 medium onions, chopped

1 can northern beans

1 can pinto beans

1 can original Rotel tomatoes

1 can petite diced tomatoes (I use the chili-ready kind)

2 cans sweet kernel corn

1 cup medium salsa

2 tsp. beef broth paste added to 2 cups of water, or 2 cups of ready-made beef broth

¼ cup Brandi's Homemade Taco Seasoning

2 tsp. additional cumin

2 tsp. additional garlic powder

Directions

1. After you defrost the meat, cook the ground beef, and chop your onion, most of the labor of this recipe is over.

2. After that, opening cans and dumping into your Crock-Pot is all that's left to do! Well, the occasional stir and sample remains, of course. Nothing has to be drained, just add it in! I choose to use different beans just to give the soup color, but if you prefer kidney beans or don't like the northern variety, use whatever two cans of beans you like best. You will need to rinse and drain the black beans if you choose them, or you will turn your soup a murky gray color—been there, done that!

3. Let your soup cook on low for 6 hours and then be ready with sour cream, shredded cheese, cilantro, guacamole, tortilla chips, or even pumpkin seeds (they really add a nice healthy crunch) for your toppings.

4. My friend Brandi has created a magical homemade taco seasoning that I highly recommend! It doesn't have the extra MSG that other seasonings have, and when doubled—or even quadrupled—it yields plenty to use for other recipes.

HOMEMADE TACO SEASONING
Brandi Carson

Ingredients

¼ cup chili powder

1½ tsp. garlic powder

1½ tsp. onion powder

1 tsp. crushed red pepper flakes (I add less because this can make it a little spicy for the kids)

1½ tsp. dried oregano

1½ tsp. paprika

1 T. cumin

1 T. kosher salt

1 tsp. black pepper

Directions

1. Mix all ingredients together in a bowl until completely incorporated.

2. Store in a Mason jar or airtight container.

The Wise Woman Loves Her Husband

GREAT BOOKS FOR FAMILY DEVOTIONS
Deb Weakly

I love the *New International Reader's Version* (Zondervan). There are many Bibles available in this version:

The Jesus Storybook Bible by Sally Lloyd-Jones (ZonderKidz)

The Picture Bible by Iva Hoth (David C. Cook)

The Child's Story Bible by Catherine F. Voss (Eerdmans)

The Action Bible by Doug Mauss (David C. Cook)

Our 24 Family Ways by Clay Clarkson (Whole Heart)

Family Nights Tool Chest series (Heritage Builders)

SEVEN-DAY JOURNEY TO A CLOSER WALK WITH JESUS FOR THE SINGLE MOM

This seven-day journey will help you establish deep roots in your relationship with God as a woman and a single mom. Spending a little time on the action item every day this week will lead to a more intimate fellowship with the Lord and a home filled with Christ's joy and peace! The topics build upon each other, so each day, you will complete the daily assignment as well as continue to build habits from the days prior. Fall more deeply in love with your Savior, and allow yourself to recognize His love for you in a whole new way as He guides you on His path of peace.

Day 1: Read

The Bible is a love letter to you from the Lord. It is astounding that the God of the universe imparted these words just for you. How very loved you are! The whole of your life can be found in Scripture: who He is, who you are, and who He has created you to be. All His promises and commands are right there in His infallible, perfect Word, and every message therein is relevant to our world today and will absolutely transform your life and your home. In Ezekiel 3:1, God tells us to eat His Word, to consume its message until it becomes the very fiber of our being. And we need to eat of it every day. If you are not in the habit of reading the Bible daily, today is the perfect day to start. Crack open your Bible and see what God has to say to you! If you need somewhere to begin, check out the Scripture lists on pages 47-48 ("Who Is He" and "Who Am I" Scriptures to Ponder pages). Take some time each day this week to look up a passage or two and write down your observations. Sink your roots deep into the soil of God's Word as you soak up the goodness of the Lord!

Day 2: Pray

Your heavenly Father loves you, my friend. He gives you everything you need to walk boldly through this life as a woman and as a mom. He wants you to trust Him to meet your needs and the needs of your children by bringing your requests before Him in prayer. Today is the perfect day to begin a prayer journal. While the Bible is God's love letter to you, let this be *your* love letter to Him! Grab a notebook, and inside its cover, write Psalm 62:8: "Trust in Him at all times, you people; pour out your hearts to Him, for God is our refuge." Make it a habit to write your prayers to the Lord each day this week and be sure to praise Him for His goodness, even in hard times. Read the description of the Lord in Revelation 4:1-11—what a glorious, awesome Father we serve! Can you believe we have been given the privilege of going before His throne, anytime, day or night, to talk to Him? This is not a gift to take lightly!

Day 3: Listen

There is a beautiful passage in 1 Kings 19:11-12 in which the Lord said, "'Go out and stand on the mountain in the presence of the LORD, for the LORD is about to pass by.' Then a great and powerful wind tore the mountains apart and shattered the rocks before the LORD, but the LORD was not in the wind. After the wind there was an earthquake, but the LORD was not in the earthquake. After the earthquake came a fire, but the LORD was not in the fire. And after the fire came a gentle whisper." The Lord spoke in that whisper. In another translation, it is written that the sound of the Lord came as a "still small voice" (1 Kings 19:12 NKJV). And that is the way He speaks to you, sweet mama. You must listen intentionally for Him. Listen for His whispers in the Scriptures and through the promptings of His Holy Spirit. Listen for His whispers of love all around you in His creation: the wind rustling through leaves at dusk, the tiny squeals of your little one. Intentionally notice and make note of His voice. Let the Lord fill your heart with His love and His promises for you today and each day to come.

Day 4: Forgive

Oh, my friend, you have a story, don't you? Most beautiful stories involve sadness of one kind or another. And your story is surely wrapped in a cloak of sadness too. But this hurt doesn't have to be carried by you, causing the poison of unforgiveness to spread throughout your heart. This hurt is best carried by your Father (Psalm 55:22). Giving your hurt, your sadness, your anger to the Lord and never picking it up again brings a supernatural peace that is so freeing. In Isaiah 61:3, God promises to give you a crown of beauty instead of ashes. Today write a letter to the Lord giving Him all the hurts you have been carrying in your heart. It is time to release those wounds to Him, dear sister. Set the letter aflame and place it in a glass. As those hurts turn to ash, pray and thank God for the crown of beauty that He has given and will continue to reveal to you. Let God pen every page in the remainder of your story. Your life is His, so live it for His glory. He has beautiful things in store!

Day 5: Lead

All children need a parent who will lead them to the foot of the cross, and as a single mom, that task can feel staggering! But the Lord has equipped you to do this and has given you instructions of how to do so in His Word. In Deuteronomy 6:5-7 God says,

> Love the LORD your God with all your heart and with all your soul and with all your strength. These commandments that I give you today are to be on your hearts. Impress them on your children. Talk about them when you sit at home and when you walk along the road, when you lie down and when you get up.

Guide your children closer to the Lord every day by reading Scripture or a devotional with them, praying, talking about the Lord, actively thanking Him together for His goodness, and noticing small miracles and love gifts from the Lord all around you. Be intentional about encouraging your children in their walk with the Lord today and begin making a plan for how you will make this a new habit in your family.

Day 6: Leave a Legacy

As you daily lead your children to the Lord, think about your life with the end in mind. What do you want to accomplish as a mom and as a follower of Jesus? My friend, you have this opportunity to leave for your family a legacy saturated in Christ and His perfect love! Pray about what God wants for you to accomplish in this life and about the qualities and character traits He would want to cultivate in your heart and the hearts of your children. One amazing item to add to your list is leaving a legacy of Scripture and prayer for your children. Today, as you read God's Word, begin underlining verses that apply to your children and write prayers and notes of Christ-centered encouragement in the margins. This will be a treasure for your children one day. If money allows, purchase an individual Bible for each of your children and fill it with your notations and prayers for them specifically. Present it to them when they leave your home as young adults. Your prayers and biblical encouragements will make an eternal impact on their lives!

Day 7: Rest

You are cherished by your Father, my friend. In Matthew 11:28, He asks you to come to Him when you are "weary and burdened, and [He] will give you rest." He even goes further in verse 29, promising that He is "gentle and humble in heart, and [in Him] you will find rest for your soul." Doesn't that sound incredible? As a single mom, however, rest is often hard to come by. Today you will practice intentionally resting your heart before the Lord. Bask in His presence as you remember the Scriptures you have read this week and ponder His absolute majesty. Trust Him with your worries today, and let your heart, soul, and mind rest in the peace that the Lord offers. If He wrote a message to you, it may sound a bit like this one to follow. Rest in His message for you today.

> My Beloved Daughter,
>
> You are so precious and honored in My sight (Isaiah 43:4). I have loved you with an everlasting love; I have drawn you with unfailing kindness (Jeremiah 31:3). I have plans to prosper you and not to harm you, plans to give you hope and a future (Jeremiah 29:11). I am faithful and true (Revelation 19:11). I will go before you and be with you; I will never ever leave you or abandon you (Deuteronomy 31:8). Because I am with you wherever you go, you do not need to be afraid or discouraged. In Me, you can be strong and courageous (Joshua 1:9)!
>
> I have set you free from the bonds of sin so that you can follow Me, and My path leads to holiness and life everlasting (Romans 6:22). You are a new creation in me, your heart-ties to sin are gone (2 Corinthians 5:17). I have given you a new heart and put a new spirit in you (Ezekiel

36:26). I have forgiven you and have given you the power to forgive others too (Ephesians 4:32). Out of love, I want you to forgive even those who have hurt you the most (Matthew 5:44-45).

Your soul is thirsty isn't it? Drink of My living water—the Holy Spirit—and your soul will never be thirsty again (John 7:37-39). Call to Me, and I will answer you and tell you great and unsearchable things you do not know (Jeremiah 33:3). Cast your cares on Me, and I will sustain you (Psalm 55:22). I am preparing a place for you (John 14:2). One day, you will be with Me, and there will be no more sorrow or pain (Revelation 21:3-4). My beloved, nothing—and I mean truly nothing—will separate you from My love (Romans 8:38-39).

Love, Your Father

CHICKEN ALFREDO
Brandi Carson

Chicken with homemade Alfredo sauce is a rich and creamy work of art that is sure to please your spouse! Sometimes simple ingredients create a masterpiece just like simple kindness can heal a wound.

Ingredients

2 or 3 large chicken breasts
olive oil
salt, pepper, garlic powder, and dried basil to taste
2 to 3 T. salted butter
2 to 3 cloves garlic, minced
1 qt. heavy cream
1 cup finely shredded Parmesan or Parmigiano-Reggiano
1 lb. cooked fettuccine

Directions

1. Cut chicken breasts in half lengthwise. Coat well with oil, salt, pepper, dried basil, and garlic powder.

2. Heat a large sauté pan or grill to medium-high heat. Add chicken and let sear on one side, turning when golden brown and half cooked. Continue cooking until chicken is done and browned on the other side.

3. While chicken is cooking, melt butter over medium heat.

4. Once butter is melted, add minced garlic for 30 seconds or until aromatic.

5. Add heavy cream, stir well, and reduce heat to medium-low.

6. Simmer, but do not allow to boil, for 20 to 30 minutes until reduced and thick, stirring occasionally. Heat may need to be reduced further to keep from boiling.

7. Boil fettuccine noodles while cooking chicken and Alfredo sauce.

8. Once the chicken is done, set aside to cool and rest.

9. Once Alfredo sauce is thickened, turn off heat, add Parmesan, stirring constantly.

10. After chicken has had a chance to rest, slice diagonally at an angle.

11. Serve Alfredo sauce over fettuccine and top with chicken slices. Enjoy!

BRUSCHETTA
Brandi Carson

Fresh is always best, especially with ripe red tomatoes and large, fragrant basil leaves. Enjoy this summertime favorite all year round!

Ingredients

4 or 5 medium vine-ripened tomatoes, finely diced
large bunch of fresh basil, destemmed and finely shredded

1 large or 2 medium garlic cloves, minced

olive oil

1 bottle (approximately 8.5 oz) balsamic vinegar (the cheap
kind is fine because it is being reduced)

salt and pepper

baguette

butter, melted

Directions

1. Make balsamic reduction first. Be warned that reducing balsamic creates a strong scent. You will want to make sure to ventilate your kitchen. Pour the entire bottle of balsamic vinegar into a small saucepan. Cook over medium heat, bringing it to a boil. Let simmer for 15 to 20 minutes, checking on it periodically. It doesn't really need to be stirred, but swirl the pan occasionally to check how thick it is getting. The amount of liquid will reduce to less than half of the original amount. You are looking for a thickened liquid that will coat the back of a spoon, stay on the spoon, and be the consistency of syrup once cooled. You need to make sure it doesn't get too thick while hot, or it will be like caramel when it's cooled down.

2. In a medium bowl, combine diced tomatoes, basil, and garlic. Drizzle a couple tablespoons of olive oil over the top. Salt and pepper to taste and then drizzle about a tablespoon of the reduced balsamic over the top. Mix well and set aside. It is best if it can marinate together for a few hours before serving.

3. Preheat your oven to 400 degrees Fahrenheit.

4. Slice baguettes at an angle ⅓" thick. Arrange them on a sheet pan in a single layer. With a basting brush, coat both sides of baguette slices with melted butter. Salt and pepper as well.

5. Bake about 5 to 6 minutes until the bottoms are slightly brown, flip all the slices over, and bake an additional 4 to 5 minutes until the other side is slightly browned.

6. Serve baguette with a spoonful of the bruschetta on top with a drizzle of the balsamic reduction over the top.

SOUTHWEST EGG ROLLS
Brandi Carson

Feeding your man good wholesome food is satisfying. My husband loves this recipe to share with friends for game night, but it's also a ridiculously easy recipe to prepare together for a night in.

Ingredients

2 medium-size chicken breasts

olive oil for sautéing

1 red bell pepper, deseeded and finely diced

1 large onion, finely diced

3 or 4 medium cloves garlic, minced

1 or 2 jalapeños, depending on how much heat you want, deseeded and finely diced

1 can or 1¼ cup homemade black beans, drained

1¼ cups frozen corn

1 can green chilies

1¼ cups frozen spinach, heated up, excess water squeezed out, diced

⅓ cup prepackaged or homemade taco seasoning

3 cups shredded Pepper Jack or Monterey Jack or a Cheddar cheese blend of your choice

10 to 15 soft-taco-size tortillas

6 to 10 cups oil for frying, or canola spray for baking

toothpicks

Directions

1. Coat chicken breast with a few tablespoons of taco seasoning, reserve the rest for later.

2. Heat grill or sauté pan to medium heat. If using a pan, add oil. Sear chicken, turning halfway, and continue cooking until it's done. Set chicken aside to rest.

3. In a large pan, heat a couple tablespoons of oil over medium heat. Add garlic and sauté for a few seconds; add onions, peppers, and jalapeños. Sauté, stirring occasionally, until vegetables are tender. Once chicken is cooled, dice finely.

4. Next, add chicken, beans, corn, green chilies, taco seasoning, and spinach and mix well.

5. Turn off heat and add cheese a little at a time. It will melt easily, get thick, and help hold it together.

6. In the center of a flat tortilla add ¼ to ⅓ cup of the mixture. Fold in sides, then roll eggrolls up, secure with a toothpick. Set aside on a sprayed sheet pan. Repeat. Once all the eggrolls are rolled, flash freeze on a sheet pan and then transfer to gallon-size freezer bags. Freeze overnight or until solid before frying or baking.

7. These can be fried or baked. For baking, spray the eggrolls completely with canola oil. Arrange evenly, without touching, on a sheet pan and bake at 375 degrees Fahrenheit for 40 to 45 minutes, turning occasionally.

8. For frying, heat oil in a large pot over medium-low heat. It's important that the oil isn't too hot or the outside will be overcooked and the inside will still be frozen. Slowly add two to three egg rolls to the heated oil. Rotate the eggrolls to cook evenly. They will need to fry for 10 to 14 minutes. To make sure the egg roll is cooked completely, poke a toothpick into the cooked tortilla, and if it goes through easily, it's done. If it has resistance in the center, cook a little longer.

9. Let cool and then slice lengthwise at a diagonal. Serve with sour cream or guacamole.

49

The Wise Woman Loves Her Children

....

DAILY DISCIPLESHIP
Tara Davis

....

Mama, here are some ideas to help you establish a time of daily discipleship with your children. This list is by no means a formula; simply use it as a jumping-off point to what God wants you to do for your kids. Keep praying and following Him, and He will show you the way.

Worship Together Through His Word

Choose a time of day to consistently practice family worship. Include your husband or make it a special time with just you and your children. Read God's Word or a children's devotional and discuss as deeply as time and your children's maturity allow.

There are so many good books on missionary stories, character qualities, and following Jesus for toddlers, kids, and teens. These things add depth to your study of God's Word. See Deb's list of Great Books for Family Devotions on page 188.

Memorize Scripture

- God's Word is like honey on our lips (Psalm 119:103). Keep something sweet on hand as a treat when practicing weekly Bible verses. Children will form a positive association with studying God's Word and hiding it in their hearts.

- Begin by memorizing the books of the Bible in song form! Googling "Wee Sing Bible books song" will lead you to great songs that will help your child memorize the books of the Old and New Testaments.

- Find a free Bible verse memorization plan for kids. There are so many good ones online.

- Songs such as those by *Seeds Family Worship* or *Songs for Saplings* make Scripture memorizing fun and easy.

- Scripture is a treasure to our souls. Reward children for memorizing verses by keeping a "treasure box" filled with little gifts.

Sing Praises

- "Make a joyful noise to the Lord" (Psalm 98:4 esv)! Sing praise songs to Jesus. Your children do not care if you have a beautiful voice, and neither does the Lord!

- Choose a hymn or praise song of the month and sing it daily together. For a fantastic children's hymn study, check out *Hymns for a Child's Heart* by Joni Erickson Tada.

- Play worship music throughout the day to keep hearts focused on the Lord.

Pray with and over Your Children

- Make a prayer jar filled with the names of people and topics to pray over. Choose a couple each day and pray together.

- Download a prayer calendar on the Voice of the Martyrs website to guide you in praying for those around the world who need Jesus.

- Pray over your children in the quiet of the night after they are asleep. Pray that they will have a heart to know God (Jeremiah 24:7), that they will be salt and light for Jesus (Matthew 5:13-16), and that they will know and show the love of their Father (1 John 4:19). There are many Scriptures to pray over your children!

- Quickly pray out loud with your children when they feel frustrated, sad, hurt, or sick. Thank God together for daily joys.

Bring God into Every Aspect of the Day

- Notice God's gifts with your children. The chirping birds, the cool breeze, the flickering flame of a candle—all are God's love gifts to us. Take it a step further by keeping a family journal to track God's little blessings.

- Encourage your children to be the hands and feet of Jesus. How can they show the love of Christ to people within your home and lives? Let them brainstorm, and help them put one plan into action each week.

- Make a "thankful chain" out of paper strips. Cut a bunch of strips out to have on hand, and each day, ask your children to write down one thing they are thankful for and add it to your chain. Choose a room to hang the chain in and see how long you can make it throughout the year.

- Share with your children what God is teaching you. They will replicate the relationship they witness you pursuing with Him.

FIVE WAYS TO PRAY FOR YOUR CHILDREN
Krystle Porter

Here are five ways you, as a busy mom, can pray:

Pray with your kids to start and end the day. As you are sitting at the breakfast table, include them in your prayers for the day. Pray that you will be the mom and helper to your husband that you want to be. Then pray for your children—that they will be filled with God's joy and be patient, kind, and good listeners! At bedtime, praise God for your day. Be intentional to find all the blessings and goodness that happened in your day and point it out to your kids! Pray for anything that is troubling any of your hearts.

Pray when your kids are fighting or not getting along. After you have finished talking to them about their behavior, pray! It is such a restorative and reconciling thing when we take our problems to God. It shows our kids that He cares about all the things that happen in their lives—even their attitudes. I always pray that God will help them to be kind and loving and remind them that Jesus calls all of us to love one another.

Pray on the go! Are you driving to the grocery store? Pray with your kids that you will all be a blessing to everyone you meet. You can pray for the fire truck going by—that they will help whoever is in need and pray for the person that they are going to help. Every time my kids see an ambulance or fire truck now, they always want to pray! Pray on the way to church that you will all soak in what God has for you that day. Pray for the homeless person you see on the street. Pray for your friends or family members you are going to visit.

Pray for your meals. I know that for my family, when life gets busy, we can easily miss this one! These prayers don't need to be long. God hears our short and sweet prayers too.

Pray with your children's leading. Ask your kids what they want to pray for. You might be wonderfully surprised at what they come up with. You will also be teaching your kids to be initiators in prayer!

PICKING A HYMN FOR YOUR CHILD

Picking a hymn for each of your children is one of the most meaningful gifts you could ever give. It will anchor them during hard times and help cast a vision for their life.

It's so simple to give this gift to your child!

Pray and ask God to give you a hymn or worship song for each of your children. Ask God why He chose this one for your child.

If your child is young, sing it to them often. If they are older and you can find the story behind the hymn, share it with your child. Explain why you think God gave this child this particular hymn. Use this as a way to encourage your child's faith and the gifts the Lord has placed inside of them. Play and sing their song together with them often. Sing it at home and in the car. Talk about it in front of your child so they will hear you say how important it is.

Print out the hymn and hang it in your child's bedroom.

Pray and ask the Lord for the child to always remember their special song as a gift from God to them. Ask Him to let it be a source of encouragement to them and help to them when they are in need.

PRAYERS FOR YOUR SPECIAL-NEEDS CHILD
Brandi Carson

Pray for your child's future. It may be scary, wondering what their future will hold, but daily entrust their future to God. "'For I know the plans I have for you,' declares the LORD, 'plans to prosper you and not to harm you, plans to give you hope and a future'" (Jeremiah 29:11).

Pray for your child to love God. We want our children not only to believe in God but also love Him and long to follow Him in their lives. "You shall love the Lord your God with all your heart and with all your soul and with all your strength and with all your mind" (Luke 10:27 ESV).

This is a great promise for moms. Second Chronicles 20:15 says, "Do not be afraid or discouraged because of this vast army. For the battle is not yours, but God's." Many times as parents we need to be reminded of that. Recognize your own personal limitations. The "vast army" is God's to defeat!

Pray for strength for your precious child. Psalm 28:6-7 says, "Praise be to the LORD, for he has heard my cry for mercy. The LORD is my strength and my shield; my heart trusts in him, and he helps me. My heart leaps for joy, and with my song I praise him."

Pray for endurance and encouragement. Believe and claim this for yourselves and your children: "May the God who gives endurance and encouragement give you the same attitude of mind toward each other that Christ Jesus had" (Romans 15:5).

THE POWERFUL SIX LIST
Mari Jo Mast

1. Relax. Make an allowance for your kids' faults because you love them (Ephesians 4:2). They are going to mess up, and it's okay. Jesus already knows, and that's why He came! Lead them to the One who gives them the power to overcome sin.

2. Be humble. Don't parent out of pride. If your kid misbehaves in public or acts up around your friends' kids, smile and tell them, "So sorry, we're trying to work on this right now." Admit it when your kids are wrong, but don't shame them.

3. Be gentle. Proverbs 15:1 (NKJV) says, "A soft answer turns away wrath, but a harsh word stirs up anger." Try not to raise your voice, and instead, try to speak gently. This totally works!

4. Be patient. James 1:19 (NLT) says, "You must all be quick to listen, slow to speak, and slow to get angry." Hear with your heart, not your head, and filter, filter, filter with love.

5. Be led by the Holy Spirit. Galatians 5:18 (NKJV) says, "But if you are led by the Spirit, you are not under the law." Wow, think about this! In the middle of a conflict, pause for a while and ask God what He thinks. Carefully listen and then obey. The Spirit gives life, but the law strengthens sin.

6. Choose to live in peace (Ephesians 4:3). Don't be worried or troubled—instead, trust God with your kids. Let the shalom of God reign in your heart!

CHORE LIST
Rachel Jones

Three to Five Years Old

Empty the plastic cups, bowls, and plates from the dishwasher.
Wipe down the front of the fridge, oven, and doors
    with a wet washcloth.
Put away toys and straighten books on the bookshelf.
Clean off the kitchen table.
Fold towels and washcloths.
Make beds.

Six to Eight Years Old

Fold and put away their own laundry.
Empty all the trash cans into a large bag.
Empty the dishwasher (except for the sharp knives).
Wipe down the countertops in the kitchen and the bathroom.
Sweep the floors.
Empty the cat's litter box (might need an older sibling's
    help for this).
Fill the pet's food and water bowls.

Nine to Twelve Years Old

Dust.
Help with meal prep.
Vacuum.
Wash dishes.
Pull weeds and tend to the garden if you have one.
Wash the windows and mirrors with glass cleaner.
Clean the sinks and toilets in the bathroom.

TWENTY-FIVE SIMPLE WAYS
TO HAVE FUN WITH YOUR KIDS!
Krystle Porter

1. Plan a surprise picnic.
2. Have a "milk and cookies night" each week for a sweet treat. Let your kids look forward to it!
3. Go on a nature hike.
4. Go for a drive through a lovely, scenic part of town with the windows down.
5. Wake up your kids with breakfast in bed.
6. Implement a "pizza and movie night." It can be homemade, store bought, or ordered in, but make a tradition out of it!
7. Bake and cook together.
8. Have a family dance party. All ages. Take turns letting each child pick a song!
9. Make homemade Play-Doh.
10. Play with your kids. Are they into sports, Legos, dolls? Get on their level, set a timer for twenty minutes, and focus entirely on them!
11. Read aloud. No matter your children's ages, this is always a favorite!
12. Go on a family bike ride or one-on-one rides with each of your kiddos.
13. Plan monthly date nights with your kids. It could be at a coffee shop, a walk around the block, out to eat, a movie— you name it. But spend quality time with them!
14. Have a pillow fight.
15. Have a monthly game night.
16. Plan a water balloon fight and let them invite a few friends.

17. Construct paper airplanes and have a competition for whose flies the farthest.

18. Go bowling.

19. Start a family book club. Choose a book to read together and discuss.

20. Have a backyard campout. Pitch your tent, roast marshmallows, and share stories.

21. Look at the stars. Gather your sleeping bags and lie out on the grass and gaze away. Find constellations together!

22. Get some ice cream at the mall and visit the pet store.

23. Play hide-and-seek in the house with the little kids and at a park with older kids. Invite friends!

24. Add notes to your children's lunch boxes.

25. Have breakfast for dinner.

CRUSTLESS CARAMELIZED ONION, BACON, AND GRUYÈRE QUICHE
Rae-Ellen Sanders

Unlike a traditional quiche Lorraine, this crustless version is healthy and gluten-free. The luxury ingredient—smoked Gruyère cheese—and the caramelized onions enhance the rich, sweet, and savory flavor of this quiche. If you're not an onion lover, please don't exclude this step. You will be surprised that sautéing the onions brings out their natural sugars, and they won't taste like the crunchy bitter vegetable you are used to. Below is a recipe that feeds 4 to 6 people.

Ingredients
½ lb. bacon
2 or 3 (1½ cups) small to medium sweet onions, sliced thin in strips
6 large eggs
1 cup heavy cream

4 oz. smoked Gruyère shredded cheese

¼ cup Parmesan cheese

2 garlic cloves, minced

1 tsp. salt

¼ tsp. nutmeg

¼ tsp. black pepper

2 tsp. balsamic vinegar

Directions

1. Preheat oven to 375 degrees.

2. Using kitchen shears, cut your raw bacon into small pieces, layer in your skillet and cook until browned (cutting your bacon will save you the step of chopping cooked bacon later).

3. Remove bacon from grease to cool and then add sliced onion to oil. Sprinkle with salt.

4. Cook for 40 minutes on medium heat, stirring often. Onions will turn a lovely brown color.

5. Add in pressed garlic and then balsamic vinegar, and cook an additional 10 minutes, stirring often. Turn off to cool.

6. In a large bowl, whisk together eggs, cream, shredded Gruyère cheese, Parmesan cheese, nutmeg, black pepper, onions, and bacon.

7. Pour into sprayed pie pan and place in oven for 30 minutes. Check with toothpick or fork.

8. When egg mixture is not jiggly, your masterpiece is finished. Serve warm and enjoy time spent with those you love.

HOMEMADE PIZZA DOUGH
Brandi Carson

Every Friday night we have a family fun night. We always start off with homemade pizza. Wash your hands and get your aprons on for this budget-friendly recipe that is full of family fun.

Ingredients

- 1 pkg. (2½ tsp.) active dry yeast
- 1 tsp. honey
- 1 cup warm water (no more than 115 degrees Fahrenheit or it will kill the yeast)
- 3 cups bread flour or all-purpose flour
- 1 tsp. kosher salt
- 1 T. extra virgin olive oil

Directions

1. In a small bowl, dissolve honey and yeast in the warm water.

2. In a stand mixer or large bowl, combine flour and salt. Mix with a dough hook attachment until well combined.

3. On low speed, combine the yeast mixture and oil with the flour mixture. Continue mixing with dough hook on low speed until the mixture comes cleanly away from the bowl. This may take up to 5 minutes.

4. Turn dough out onto a clean surface and knead by hand for a few minutes or until the dough is firm and smooth.

5. Oil a large bowl and place the dough in the bowl. Flip the dough so it is well coated with oil. Cover with plastic wrap and let rise for 30 to 45 minutes or until doubled in size.

6. Preheat your oven to 450 degrees Fahrenheit.

7. When the dough is ready to make into a pizza, cut it in half for smaller pizzas or make one large pizza.

8. Dust work surface lightly with flour and roll dough with a pizza roller or spread it out with your fingers.

9. Add sauce and toppings as desired and top with cheese.

10. Bake 12 to 18 minutes, depending on the thickness of your crust and the size of your pizza.

50

The Wise Woman Creates a Home

THE WISE WOMAN BUILDS HER HOUSE
Tara Davis

"The wise woman builds her house" (Proverbs 14:1).

A beautiful house is not just slapped together haphazardly: a wall here, a paint sample there, maybe a stair or two in the corner. Building a beautiful house requires a great deal of planning. The same is true with our life and our family. We cannot expect to have a beautiful family and a home filled with the love of Jesus without consistent intentionality.

Proverbs 24:3-4 tells us, "By wisdom a house is built, and through understanding it is established; through knowledge its rooms are filled with rare and beautiful treasures." God has given you the special privilege of building your home, your family environment, for Him. Just as a builder needs a blueprint to create a good home, you need a plan of action as well.

What characteristics do you want your home to have? With which qualities will you fill the rooms? Will you decorate with kindness, worship, beauty, patience, joy, discipleship, faith, self-discipline, service, encouragement, and prayer?

Take some time today to sit and jot down in your journal specific qualities you would like to fill your home and any Scripture that would relate. Mama, be intentional about building the home in which your family will thrive and bring glory to the Lord!

HOMEMADE LAUNDRY DETERGENT
Brandi Carson

Saving money is always on my mind, being a mom of a large family. This recipe yields six months of laundry detergent for less than $20!

Ingredients
1 (4 lb.) box baking soda
1 (55 oz.) box super washing soda laundry booster
1 (4 lb.) box Borax
2 bottles scent booster, like Purex Crystals or Downy Unstoppables
3 bars Ivory Soap

Directions
1. Cut each bar of soap into six pieces and place two to three pieces on a plate or in a bowl. Microwave in batches for 30 seconds each. The soap will grow into a large soap cloud.

2. Let your kids join in the fun! Take soap out of the microwave, let it cool for a minute, and let them crumble it into a garbage bag.

3. Add all remaining ingredients to the garbage bag, hold the top closed, and shake and roll the bag around to mix the ingredients.

4. Pour into a container and use about ¼ cup for a large load of laundry. Use a couple of tablespoons for a smaller load.

SCONES
Brandi Carson

What is more beautiful than sitting around a table with a good, hot cup of coffee (or tea) and delicious scones? This is a great recipe that you can customize with any flavor filling. Make the dough ahead of time, freeze it, and then bake the scones hot and fresh whenever you want!

Ingredients

2½ cups all-purpose flour
¼ cup sugar
1 tsp. salt
2 tsp. baking powder
½ tsp. baking soda
½ cup unsalted butter, chilled and diced
¾ cup half-and-half
¼ to ½ cup mix-ins, such as chocolate chips, raisins with cinnamon, apples, blueberries, orange zest…the possibilities are endless!

Directions

1. In a mixing bowl, whisk together dry ingredients.
2. Add chilled butter. Using your hands or pastry blender, cut in butter until flour mixture is a crumbly coarse texture.
3. In a separate bowl, add your mix-ins and about ¼ cup of flour mixture. Coat mix-ins well with flour mixture. This will help the mix-ins stick to the dough well.
4. Add coated mix-ins to flour mixture. Stir well to combine.
5. Add half-and-half and stir in gently until combined. Dump onto a floured countertop and knead until flour is well combined. The less you mix the dough, the more tender the scones will be.

6. Be sure the countertop is still well floured and roll dough out to about 1- to 1½-inch thickness and shaped like a rectangle or square. Cut dough into long rows and then cut each row into individual triangles. You could also make round scones by cutting them with a biscuit cutter. Gather scraps and repeat. Makes 20 to 25 small scones or a dozen larger ones.

7. For best results, chill scones for at least half an hour or freeze them before baking. Cold butter results in tender, flakier scones. In an oven preheated to 400 degrees Fahrenheit, bake large scones for 12 to 15 minutes, smaller scones for 8 to 10 minutes. Scones with fresh fruit tend to need to bake longer because of the moisture in them.

8. Dust with powdered sugar, or make a simple glaze to drizzle on top. Serve.

WAFFLES
Brandi Carson

Waffles make breakfast or even dinner fun! Most of all, the variety of toppings is what makes them delicious and memorable!

Ingredients

3 cups all-purpose flour
2 tsp. salt
1 tsp. baking soda
2 eggs
1 cup granulated sugar
4 T. butter, softened
4 T. shortening
1 cup half-and-half
1 cup milk
½ cup buttermilk
½ tsp. vanilla

Directions

1. Preheat waffle iron while making batter.

2. Combine flour, salt, and baking soda in a medium bowl. Whisk together until well combined.

3. In a stand mixer or large bowl with a hand mixer, cream together shortening, butter, and sugar until creamy.

4. Add one egg at a time and blend thoroughly until light and creamy.

5. In a separate bowl, mix together milk, half-and-half, buttermilk, and vanilla.

6. Add half of the liquid mixture to the creamed butter mixture and mix until well combined, scraping the bowl after each addition.

7. Add half of the flour mixture to the creamed butter mixture and mix until well combined, again scraping the bowl after each addition. Repeat steps 6 and 7 with the remainder of the creamed butter mixture and remainder of flour mixture.

8. Use a scoop or measuring cup to pour the required amount of batter onto waffle iron and cook until golden brown. Cooking time and amount of batter needed will vary with different waffle irons.

9. Serve hot with your favorite toppings, or freeze extras for later.

51

The Wise Woman Fosters Friendships

SUPER SUCCULENT CARROT CAKE
Rae-Ellen Sanders

There is no better combo, in my opinion, than moist carrot cake and heavenly cream cheese frosting! This labor of love is sure to win hearts.

Ingredients

2 cups flour
2 cups sugar
2½ tsp. cinnamon
½ tsp. nutmeg
2 tsp. baking soda
1 tsp. salt
1½ cups vegetable oil
3 cups shredded carrots
1 to 2 T. water (if using packaged shredded carrots)
4 eggs
2 tsp. vanilla
milk

Directions

1. Sift your flour and sugar. I promise it is worth the time to do this!

2. Add the remaining dry ingredients.

3. Slowly add the oil, whisking fervently until well blended. It might seem like this is way too much oil, but trust me, it is the secret to how moist and delicious this cake is!

4. Place carrots into the food processor and chop to a fine texture. Increase liquid by adding 1 to 2 T. of water if using preshredded variety.

5. Using a hand mixer, mix the eggs and vanilla into the batter.

6. Next, combine your carrots and fold it all in. Voila!

7. Pour the batter into two prepared, greased cake pans of the same size. *Tip*: Use wax paper cut to fit inside your pans for an easy release.

8. Bake at 350 degrees Fahrenheit for 40 to 45 minutes.

9. Test with fork to make sure it comes out clean.

10. Let cool completely before frosting.

HEAVENLY CREAM CHEESE FROSTING

Now for the irresistible creamy cream cheese frosting! Soften the cream cheese and butter by placing them in a bowl on your counter before you start mixing your cake batter. Do not microwave to soften. Philadelphia Cream Cheese blends more easily than other varieties. Very importantly, make sure to use full-fat butter, not margarine.

I have doubled this frosting recipe because you will apply a nice, thick layer between the cakes and a generous layer on top. If you think it is too much frosting, feel free to cut the ingredients in half. You are creating greatness here—so don't worry about the calories until you are on your second piece!

Ingredients

2 (16 oz.) pkgs. cream cheese, softened

1 stick (½ cup) butter, softened

4 tsp. vanilla

2 lbs. powdered sugar

2 T. milk

Directions

1. Using a hand mixer, blend cream cheese, butter, and vanilla together. Slowly add in the powdered sugar until thick and creamy. Add milk as needed for desired texture. This is sweet, but it complements the carrot cake perfectly!

2. Spread enough frosting around the tops and sides of both cakes to hold down any crumbs.

3. Place in fridge or freezer for 20 minutes to set.

4. Take out and place the bottom layer on a special plate or cake platter. Add a good amount of frosting to create a yummy middle layer and top with the other cake.

5. Frost the sides and top. Decorate with shelled and chopped walnuts or pecans pressed into the sides (optional). Indulge!

Notes

1. E.M. Bounds, *The Possibilities of Prayer* (Grand Rapids, MI: New Christian Classics Library, 2018), 27.

2. See John Piper, "What Is Hope?," Desiring God, April 6, 1986, https://www.desiringgod.org/messages/what-is-hope.

3. Mark Batterson, *The Circle Maker* (Grand Rapids, MI: Zondervan, 2016), 20.

4. Stormie Omartian, *The Power of a Praying Wife* (Eugene, OR: Harvest House, 1997).

About the Authors

*Dear sister, thank you so much for reading our book.
Now we'd like to share a little bit about ourselves.*

....

Deb Weakly

I helped create the Help Club for Moms with one goal in mind: to create a community in which moms help moms to know the love of Christ. If there is one thing I would love to share with you, it is that God is personal and loves you as you are. You don't have to be perfect to be loved by our amazing God!

My husband, Randy, and I have been married for twenty-eight years, and we have two grown children, Christie and Jack, and one answer-to-prayer son-in-law named Alex. And now I get to be a Gigi to my sweet little grandbaby, Aspen! Yay!

Mari Jo Mast

I have been with the Help Club for Moms since its beginning, and I can't tell you how blessed I am because of this loving, growing community. I enjoy writing Bible studies and penning posts on Thursday mornings on Facebook. My husband and I have seven beautiful children (three of them are married now). I absolutely adore spending time with our four precious grandchildren. I greatly treasure my family. I consider nothing more important than working in tandem with the kingdom of God, having a relationship with Jesus, and listening to the Holy Spirit. The Word of God feeds my soul and lights my path every single day. The knowledge of Jesus living in me has changed my life.

Kristall Willis

I'm mama to two beautiful children (whom I home-school and who also drive me a little bit crazy) and wife to my handsome husband, Luke, whom I've been married to for more than ten years. Luke is my strength when I'm weak, and we complement each other in such different ways. I'm blessed to design and lay out all the Help Club for Moms books, utilizing my background in graphic design. My journey has taken me to a place I never imagined, both physically and spiritually. I now reside in Colorado Springs, but I am originally from the DC area. I try to lead a Spirit-led life, building my faith throughout the ups and downs and trusting God along the way!

Krystle Porter

Over the years being with this ministry, I have grown deeper in my relationship with Jesus, and it's given me a sweet sisterhood and faith community! It has been a true blessing.

I have been married to my husband for fourteen years, and our children are ages ten, eight, six, four, and almost two! Three girls and two boys. Motherhood has been the most refining work in my life thus far, but there is also so much beauty in it!

I am a firm believer in honoring Jesus by enjoying this life He has given us. Trying to find beauty and goodness in the mundane places of life, I feel, is the calling of my heart!

Jennifer Valdois

I have been married to the love of my life, Todd, for more than twenty years. We have one lovely daughter and two delightful sons. In my free time, I enjoy gardening and camping with my family. My faith in Jesus Christ has been a lifelong journey, striving to know Him and His love and forgiveness. I am so grateful to be able to share that love through the Help Club for Moms.

Brandi Carson

I'm mama of five crazy kiddos. We have lived in Colorado for the last several years but had quite a long journey to get here. My husband's job moved us around to four different states in two years. We plan on being here for a while, but we never know what adventure God has in store for us. I am a money-saving, deal-finding, DIY-crafting lover of coffee and dark chocolate. I love being a mom, wife, and homemaker. Cooking for people is how I show them love, and I use this passion with the Help Club for Moms by writing recipes for our books. I love being a part of this amazing community that God has placed me in and learning from so many different mamas in so many different seasons of life.

Tara Davis

I'm a mama to three wild, wonderful boys on earth (and one tiny boy in heaven) and wife to one handsome husband for sixteen years. When you see someone has had a hand in writing a book for moms, you immediately assume they must have it all together. I do not. Maybe you don't either. But I have some good news for you—we have a perfectly gracious Savior who loves us so very much, imperfections and all! Together, we can learn who He is and who we are in Him. Together, we can take this one little life He has given us and pour out His love in a way that changes hearts, especially our own!

Rachel Jones

I am so excited to meet you! Thank you for reading our book. I am a normal mama just like you. I have one wonderful husband and four crazy and joyful children—three big girls and one little boy. I am originally from the desert in Arizona, and now I live in the beautiful mountains of Colorado. I homeschool our children and struggle every day. Being a part of Help Club for Moms has been a blessing in my life, and I truly couldn't mother without this incredible community behind me.

Rae-Ellen Sanders

I'm a lover of Jesus, coffee, books, and friends. I'm blessed to be married to an amazing husband who loves the Lord. We raise a quiver of five children ranging from six to eighteen. God brought me to this wonderful ministry after leaving a career as a flight attendant. I'm grateful for the Help Club for Moms challenge to put God first and to be the best mom I can be through the power of the Holy Spirit! I need this community of moms cheering me on to run this race of motherhood while fixing my eyes on Jesus. I'm so thankful God brought you to our group too.

Melissa Lain

I am the wife to an amazing man, Larry, my high school sweetheart, whose servant-leadership has made me a better woman. We have two amazingly active children in their twenties. As a young mom and wife, I realized the blessing of older women in my life. I am praying for you—dear wife, mom, precious child of God—that Help Club for Moms is a community where you experience the love of our Savior so that you will make an eternal impact on those within and without your four walls. Allow us to take you by the hand to instruct, guide, and encourage you in this season of motherhood.

About Help Club for Moms

....

Help Club for Moms is a group of moms who seek to grow closer to Jesus, closer to our families, and closer to each other. We believe prayer changes everything and Jesus is big enough to help us raise the children with whom God has blessed us.

We focus on digging into God's Word, praying together, and encouraging one another! Through weekly Mom Tips and daily Faith-Filled Ideas, the Help Club for Moms helps women take what they are learning about the Lord and apply it to their daily journey as wives and mothers. Our goal is to spread the love of Jesus, inspire women to be the wives and mothers God created us to be, and to impact eternity—one mama at a time!

Would you like to be a part of this community? Here's how you can get involved in the Help Club for Moms:

- Purchase our books on Amazon. We use 100 percent of the proceeds to fund our all-volunteer ministry. The titles include *The Wise Woman Knows, The Wise Woman Loves, The Wise Woman Stays, The Wise Woman Abides, The Wise Woman Grows, The Wise Woman Enjoys,* and *The Joy Challenge for Moms.*

- Pray for the ministry and the moms in our Help Club for Moms community worldwide—for them to know the love of Jesus and create a Christlike atmosphere in their homes.

- Start a Help Club for Moms group at your local church or home. We can help you!

- We are always on the lookout for Titus 2 women who can help mentor our moms through social media and prayer.

- If you are an author, blogger, graphic artist, or social media guru, we need you and your talents at the Help Club for Moms!

- We are a 501(c)(3) and an all-volunteer ministry. Visit www .HelpClubForMoms.com to help us get God's Word into the hands of moms worldwide!

Questions? Email us at
info@helpclubformoms.com
You can find out more about Help Club for Moms at
www.HelpClubForMoms.com
and on Facebook and Instagram
@HelpClubForMoms

ALSO FROM THE HELP CLUB FOR MOMS...

If you want to grow deeper in your walk with Christ, thrive in your relationships, and be inspired on your daily journey as a woman, wife, and mother, we have the perfect tool for you! *The Help Club for Moms Companion Guide* is a beautiful Bible study journal that partners with *The Help Club for Moms* book to help you walk through Scripture and seek the Lord in prayer. In addition to Bible study helps and journal prompts, you'll find a code to access encouraging videos, dozens of free printables, and membership to an exclusive online club!

This helpful resource also makes it easy to bring *The Help Club for Moms* book to your church or women's group as an interactive, Scripture-rich Bible study. Find *The Help Club for Moms Companion Guide* on Amazon.